THE FIBRE COOKBOOK

Elisabeth Lambert Ortiz started
has lived and worked as a journ
including her native England, i
Caribbean, and the Far East, in ~~~~~~ ~~~ ~~~~~~ ~~~~~~~~ ~~~ ~~
Australia. She is at present living in London with her Mexican
husband, Cesar Ortiz-Tinoco.

Mrs Ortiz is one of the few food writers with direct knowledge and
practical experience of cooking in both hemispheres and in four of the
five continents (she has also visited the fifth). She is the prize-winning
author of a number of ethnic cookbooks and has been called a food
historian and a culinary anthropologist, but describes herself simply as
a food writer, though her researches into a cuisine include
investigations of the remote past as well as journeys into the present.

Her books include: *The Complete Book of Mexican Cooking; Caribbean Cooking;
The Complete Book of Japanese Cooking; Cooking with the Young Chefs of France*
and *The Book of Latin American Cooking*.

THE FISH COOKBOOK

...d to travel with her family as a child and
...st journalist and writer all over the world
...n the United States, Mexico, the
...South and Central America and in

THE FIBRE COOKBOOK

Elisabeth Lambert Ortiz

Jill Norman & Hobhouse

Jill Norman & Hobhouse Ltd
Gloucester Mansions, Cambridge Circus, London WC2

First published by Jill Norman & Hobhouse, 1982
Copyright © Elisabeth Lambert Ortiz, 1982

Decorations in the text are taken from
Modern Cookery for Private Families by Eliza Acton
and *Mrs Beeton's Book of Household Management*

Typeset by V & M Graphics Ltd, Aylesbury, Bucks
Printed and bound in Great Britain by Mackays of Chatham Ltd

Contents

PREFACE	6
SOUPS	8
FISH	20
MEAT AND POULTRY	30
VEGETABLES	40
BEANS, RICE AND GRAINS	57
SALADS	72
BREAD AND CAKES	84
DESSERTS	94
SAUCES, PICKLES AND SAVOURIES	99
FIBRE CHART	105
INDEX	111

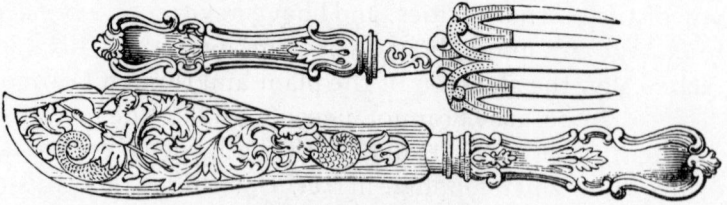

Preface

No one talked about complex carbohydrates or fibre-rich foods when I was growing up, but my mother saw to it that we had plenty of what we called roughage in our diet. Apples, and other fruit like plums, were washed and eaten with the skin on, and we had two or three green vegetables at dinner every day. At least once a week we had home cooked beans, sometimes butter beans, sometimes kidney beans. We had brown lentils quite often, and were given dried fruits if we wanted something sweet. My mother, who was a very good cook, would not have 'balloon' bread in the house, and she baked once a week so that shop-bought cakes were unknown to us. When we lived for a few years in Jamaica we had a very good cook, and as a result our culinary horizons widened. We learned to enjoy rice and beans among other things. And since we were, on both sides, rather a travelling family, new ideas and new foods were constantly introduced into the repertoire. Mother was not a food faddist, she was just sensible, and knowledgeable. I've always enjoyed the complex carbo-hydrates whatever name they go under, fibre, or roughage, and meals without them would be dull things indeed, as this small collection of recipes is designed to show.

We were brought up to think of the need for roughage as one of the eternal verities, and I have never seen any need to change my mind about this. I am aware that fibre is, technically, the skeleton of the plant and though I cannot digest it, or because I cannot digest it, vital to the health of my digestive process. It supplies the bulk I need, but I must confess that when I indulge in freshly gathered field mushrooms the fact that they are almost entirely composed of indigestible cellulose is not what I have in mind. The taste of the delicious things is what matters.

We are not in the habit of thinking out the end result of breakfast, lunch or dinner when we sit down to eat. Nor should we. If we eat the right foods that will all be taken care of naturally. Foods rich in fibre are all the unrefined cereals, nuts and seeds and legumes, fresh vegetables and fruits and dried fruits. It gives a very wide choice.

Bon appétit ought to mean a good appetite for the right things, things that are good for us, and that taste good too.

Elisabeth Lambert Ortiz

Soups

There are few things in this life as pleasant as a bowl of thick hearty soup in cold winter weather for lunch or dinner, or of a light, delicate, chilled soup to stimulate the appetite in hot summer. Fortunately both types of soup are almost certain to be rich in fibre, and so in addition to everything else, good for you. With the addition of an unrefined cereal bread and fresh or dried fruit for dessert, nothing more is needed for a satisfying meal.

BEAN AND CABBAGE SOUP

It has been said of this soup that it should be thick enough for a spoon to stand up in it. Whether true or not, it is certain that winter nights were created so that this soup could be served. Freshly baked wholemeal bread is a fine accompaniment.

Serves 6 to 8

> 1 lb/450 g white haricot beans
> 1 large onion, chopped
> 2 cloves garlic, chopped
> bouquet garni tied in a square of cheesecloth
> 3 sprigs parsley, sprig or ½ teaspoon thyme,
> 1 clove, and 1 bay leaf
> 1½ lb/700 g smoked ham hocks
> 1 lb/450 g potatoes, peeled and sliced
> 1 medium-sized cabbage, halved, cored and shredded
> ½ lb/225 g carrots, scraped and sliced
> ½ lb/225 g turnips, peeled and cubed
> 1 lb/450 g green beans cut into small pieces
> salt, freshly ground pepper

Rinse and pick over the beans. Put the beans into a large saucepan or soup kettle with cold water to cover and bring to the boil, covered, over moderate heat. Simmer for 5 minutes. Turn off the heat and let the beans stand for 1 hour. Drain and cover with fresh water. Add the onion, garlic, bouquet garni and ham hocks and simmer, covered, for 1 hour. Add all the remaining ingredients and 3½ pints/2 litres water and simmer until all the vegetables are tender. Remove and discard the bouquet garni. Lift out the ham hocks. Peel off the rind and cut the meat into chunks. Discard the rind and bone. Return the meat to the soup. If necessary add a little more water and heat the soup through. Taste for seasoning and add salt and pepper if necessary. Serve with plenty of freshly baked wholemeal bread and butter or margarine. Serve in large soup bowls.

BLACK BEAN SOUP

This hearty soup takes well to being reheated and will keep, refrigerated, for up to a week. Add a sandwich made with bran or wholemeal bread for a delectable fibre-rich lunch.

Serves 8 to 10

    1 lb/450 g black kidney beans
    1 oz/30 g butter
    2 medium onions, finely chopped
    2 medium stalks celery, chopped
    4 sprigs parsley, sprig thyme, 1 bayleaf tied up in a square
        of cheesecloth
    2 pints/1.1 litre beef stock
    2 pints/1.1 litre water
    salt, freshly ground pepper
    for the garnish: chopped hard-boiled egg, chopped parsley
        and lemon slices

Put the beans into a large saucepan with cold water to cover and bring to the boil, covered, over moderate heat. Simmer for 5 minutes. Remove from the heat and allow to stand for 1 hour. Drain, rinse and set the beans aside.

In a frying pan heat the butter and sauté the onions and celery over low heat until the onion is soft. Add the onion mixture, the bouquet garni, the stock, water and salt and pepper to taste to the drained beans. Simmer the beans in a covered pan over moderate heat, stirring from time to time, until they are very soft, about 1½ to 2 hours. Remove and discard the cheesecloth bag. Purée the solids in a food processor or blender, or put through the medium disc of a food mill. Return the purée to the soup. Taste for seasoning and add more salt and pepper if necessary. Reheat gently and serve garnished with a slice of lemon sprinkled with chopped egg and parsley.

LENTIL AND DRIED APRICOT SOUP

Serves 6

    8 oz/225 g brown lentils
    4 oz/100 g dried apricots
    1 tablespoon olive or vegetable oil
    1 medium onion, finely chopped
    1 clove garlic, chopped

2 pints/1.1 litre chicken stock
salt, freshly ground pepper
½ teaspoon ground cardamom
¼ pint/150 ml single cream or plain yoghurt
garnish: chopped parsley, fresh coriander, mint leaves, or
    lemon balm leaves or snipped chives

Put the lentils into a large saucepan with cold water to cover. Bring to the boil, covered, over moderate heat. Remove from the heat and stand, covered, for 1 hour. Drain. Transfer to a bowl. Rinse out and dry the saucepan. While the lentils are soaking put the apricots into a bowl with warm water to cover and soak for 30 minutes. Drain and chop.

Heat the oil in the saucepan, add the onion and sauté until it is soft. Add the garlic and sauté for 1 or 2 minutes longer. Add the lentils and the apricots. Pour in the chicken stock, season to taste with salt and pepper. Stir in the cardamom. Bring to the boil over moderate heat, and simmer, covered, over low heat for 45 minutes or until the lentils are very soft. Purée the solids in a food processor or blender. Return the purée to the saucepan, stir in the cream and heat through. Serve hot, garnished with any preferred herb.

Variation: Omit the cream. Let the soup cool after puréeing the solids. Stir in the yoghurt. Chill thoroughly and serve cold garnished with mint or coriander.

LENTIL SOUP

For a more conventional lentil soup and one that is comforting in cold winter weather this is a simple recipe that needs little attention.

Serves 6 to 8

  1 oz/30 g butter or oil
  2 medium onions, finely chopped
  2 medium carrots, scraped and chopped
  3 stalks celery, chopped
  8 oz/225 g brown lentils
  1¾ pints/1 litre beef or chicken stock
  1¾ pints/1 litre water
  salt, freshly ground pepper
  parsley, finely chopped

Heat the butter in a large saucepan and sauté the onions, carrots and celerey over low heat until the vegetables are soft. Add the lentils, stir, add the stock and water and salt and pepper to taste. Bring to the boil, cover and simmer over low heat, stirring from time to time until the lentils are very soft and disintegrating into the liquid. The time will vary according to the type of lentil but it is usually about 1 hour. Purée the solids in a food processor or blender and return to the saucepan. Taste for seasoning and add salt and pepper if necessary. Serve in a tureen, sprinkled with the parlsey.

Variations: Many legumes lend themselves to the same treatment as lentils in this soup. Red or green lentils can be used, and so can yellow or green split peas. The flavour will differ in subtle ways but that is all. Non-dieters may like to stir in a tablespoon or so of unsalted butter as an enrichment, or perhaps a little soured cream. Herbs other than parsley can be used as a garnish according to individual taste.

GALICIAN BEAN SOUP
Caldo Gallego

I was given this recipe for Caldo Gallego years ago by a

Galician friend. It is a soup I have always enjoyed and it has the added merit of being high in fibre. I leave the potatoes unpeeled.

Serves 6

> ½ lb/225 g dried white haricot beans
> 4 lb/100 g smoked ham in one piece
> 4 lb/100 g salt pork or lean smoked bacon in one piece
> 3½ pints/2 litres water
> 1 medium onion, finely chopped
> ½ medium cabbage, chopped
> 4 small white turnips, peeled and quartered
> ½ lb/225 g spring greens, or turnip greens, chopped
> 4 medium potatoes, scrubbed and quartered
> ½ lb/225 g chorizo or any smoked garlic sausage

Wash and pick over the beans. Rinse them in cold water. Put them into a large saucepan with cold water to cover and bring to the boil over high heat. Boil for 2 minutes. Remove from the heat and stand, covered, for 1 hour. Drain, discarding the soaking water. Add the smoked ham and salt pork or bacon to the pot with 3½ pints/2 litres water and simmer for 1½ hours. Add the onion, cabbage, turnips, spring greens or turnip greens, potatoes and sausage and simmer for 30 minutes longer. Taste the soup and season with salt and pepper. Lift out the meats and sausage and cut them into bite-size pieces. Return them to the saucepan. Serve in large soup bowls accompanied by bran bread, or wholemeal bread.

Variation: Instead of haricot beans, use chickpeas. Omit the cabbage and spring greens and add ½ lb/225 g sliced courgettes, ½ lb/225 g green beans cut into small pieces, 2 cloves garlic, crushed, ¼ teaspoon ground saffron and a generous amount of freshly ground pepper. Add these to the soup in the last 20 minutes of cooking. Five minutes before the soup is ready stir in 1 oz/25 g chopped parsley.

MINESTRONE
Mixed Vegetable Soup

This is a soup that combines many fibre virtues, which may explain why it is the most famous of the vegetable soups. Green vegetables, rice and dried beans all add their fibre quota to this delicious soup, which is good at any time but is perfect for serving at the end of a late night party. Whole wheat pasta may be used instead of the brown rice used in this recipe.

Serves 6 to 8

4 tablespoons olive oil
1 medium onion, finely chopped
1 leek, well washed, using white part only, chopped
1 clove garlic, chopped
bouquet garni: 3 parsley sprigs, 1 bay leaf, sprig rosemary, sprig thyme tied together with cotton, or tied in a square of cheesecloth
½ lb/225 g tomatoes, peeled and chopped
4 celery stalks, chopped
2 medium sized carrots, scraped and diced
2 medium sized potatoes, peeled and diced
4 oz/100 g courgettes, diced
4 oz/100 g peas
4 oz/100 g green beans, cut into 1 inch/2.5 cm pieces
4 pints/2.3 litres chicken or beef stock
½ small cabbage, shredded
4 oz/100 g brown rice *OR*
4 oz/100 g whole wheat spaghetti, broken into 1 inch/2.5 cm pieces
6 oz/175 g dried haricot, or cannellini beans, cooked
salt, freshly ground pepper
freshly grated Parmesan cheese

In a large saucepan or soup kettle heat the oil. Add the onion, leek and garlic and sauté over moderate heat until the onion and leek are soft. Add the bouquet garni, tomatoes, celery, carrots, potatoes, courgettes, peas, green beans and sauté for a few minutes. Pour in the stock, cover and simmer over moderate heat for 35 minutes or until the vegetables are cooked. They should not be mushy. Add the cabbage, rice or spaghetti and the cooked dried beans. Season to taste with salt and pepper and simmer until the rice is tender, about 15 minutes. Remove and discard the bouquet garni. Serve in large soup bowls with grated cheese.

SORREL SOUP

This vegetable soup has all the goodness of mixed root vegetables together with the delicate flavour of sorrel.

Serves 6 to 8

> 2 oz/50g butter
> 1 large or 2 medium onions, finely chopped
> 1/4 lb/100 g each scraped and chopped carrot, turnip and
>   parsnip
> 1 lb/450 g potatoes, peeled and cubed
> 1½ pints/850 ml beef or chicken stock
> 1 recipe plain chiffonnade of sorrel (page 55)
> salt, freshly ground pepper

In a large, heavy saucepan heat the butter and sauté the onion until it is soft. Add the carrot, turnip and parsnip and sauté for 3 or 4 minutes longer. Add the potatoes, and stir to mix. Pour in the stock, bring to a simmer and cook over low heat until the vegetables are tender, about 30 minutes. Stir in the sorrel, season to taste with salt and pepper and simmer for 5 minutes longer.

The soup may be garnished, if liked, with chopped hardboiled egg, fresh dill or chives and a spoonful of soured cream.

FRESH PEA SOUP

Serves 8

1 oz/25 g butter
1 large onion, finely chopped
2 lb/900 g shelled fresh green peas, or frozen peas
 thoroughly defrosted
1¾ pts/1 litre chicken stock
salt, freshly ground pepper
2 oz/50 g mint leaves, chopped
plain yoghurt (optional)
small mint sprigs for garnish

Heat the butter in a saucepan and sauté the onion over low heat until it is soft. Add the peas and the stock, cover and simmer over low heat until the peas are tender, about 10 minutes. Purée the solids in a blender or food processor, or put through a food mill. Return them to the liquid. Season the soup with salt and pepper and serve either hot or chilled, garnished with a sprig of mint. If serving the soup chilled it may be garnished also with a spoonful of plain yoghurt.

TURNIP SOUP

Young white turnips make a delicious soup adding to the pleasures of springtime.

Serves 6

1½ lb/700 g young, white turnips, peeled and sliced
1¼ pints/700 ml milk
1¼ pints/700 ml chicken stock
salt, white pepper

Combine the turnips, milk, stock and salt and pepper in a large saucepan, bring to a boil, lower the heat and simmer gently, covered, until the turnips are very tender, about 25

minutes. Remove the turnips from the soup and purée
them in a blender or food processor. Return the purée to
the liquid and taste for seasoning. Add salt and pepper if
necessary. Heat the soup through.

CHILLED SUMMER SOUPS
CHILLED CORN AND TOMATO SOUP

A chilled soup can admirably stimulate the appetite and set
the tone for a summer supper, after a warm day when the
late light lingers.

Serves 6

>   1¼ pints/700 ml chicken stock
>   1 lb/450 g corn kernels, if frozen, thoroughly defrosted
>   1 lb/450 g tomatoes, peeled and chopped
>   1 onion, chopped
>   1 bay leaf
>   salt, freshly ground pepper
>   *Garnish:* finely chopped parsley or any favourite herb

Combine all the ingredients in a saucepan and simmer for
15 minutes. Remove and discard the bay leaf. Purée the
solids in a blender or food processor and return to the
liquid. Stir to mix and cool.

Chill the soup until ready to serve. Pour into soup bowls
and garnish with chopped herbs.

GREEN SUMMER SOUP
Serves 6

>   2 pints/1.1 litre chicken stock
>   ½ lb/225 g green beans, chopped
>   1 small cos lettuce, chopped
>   ½ lb/225 g courgettes, chopped

¾ lb/330 g peas, if frozen, thoroughly defrosted
½ lb/225 g chopped celery
1 leek, white part only, thoroughly washed and chopped
3 spring onions with some of the green, chopped
2 oz/50 g parsley, preferably flat type
salt, freshly ground pepper
6 slices hardboiled egg

Combine all the ingredients except the hardboiled egg in a saucepan and bring to a simmer. Simmer, covered, for 15 minutes or until all the vegetables are tender. Lift out and purée the solids in a blender or food processor. Return to the liquid, put in a bowl and chill the soup thoroughly. Serve garnished with a slice of hardboiled egg.

COLD CARROT SOUP

Serves 6

1 lb/450 g carrots, scraped and coarsely chopped
1½ pints/850 ml chicken stock
1 medium onion, finely chopped
½ oz/15 g butter
1 tablespoon curry powder
8 fl oz/225 ml coconut milk made by diluting creamed
 coconut to the consistency of milk
salt, freshly ground pepper
6 lemon slices

Put the carrots and chicken stock into a saucepan, bring to the boil, cover and simmer until the carrot is tender, about 25 minutes.

In a small frying pan heat the butter and sauté the onion until it is soft. Add the curry powder and sauté for 2 or 3 minutes longer. Purée the carrots, onion and curry mixture and stir it back into the stock. Season to taste with salt and pepper and simmer gently for 10 minutes. Cool and stir in the coconut milk. Chill and serve garnished with lemon slices.

CHILLED PEANUT SOUP

Serves 6

2 pints/1.1 litre beef stock
4 oz/125 g peanuts, finely ground
1 medium onion, finely chopped
1 small fresh hot red chilli pepper, left whole (optional)
salt, freshly ground pepper
8 fl oz/225 ml plain yoghurt
sweet paprika

In a saucepan combine the beef stock, peanuts, onion, and hot pepper and simmer, covered, for 15 minutes. Take out and discard the chilli pepper. Season the soup with salt and pepper and let it cool. Stir in the yoghurt. Chill the soup thoroughly. Serve sprinkled with a little sweet paprika.

Variation: For Creole Peanut soup sauté a finely chopped onion in 2 tablespoons peanut oil until soft. Add a clove of garlic, minced, and sauté for a minute or two longer. Add ¾ pint/400 ml each chicken stock and tomato juice and 4 oz/125 g peanuts, finely ground, ½ teaspoon celery seed, and salt and freshly ground pepper to taste. Cook, stirring, at just under a simmer until the soup is smooth and the flavours blended. Serve hot sprinkled with chopped parsley or fresh coriander, or chill. *Serves 4.*

Fish

Fish is not high fibre but it does lend itself to many high-fibre recipes, and besides, it has its own nutritional virtues. Fish lovers tired of plain grilled, fried or poached fish may find some appetizing ideas in this small selection of fish and shellfish recipes.

OKRA AND BANANA WITH PRAWNS

Serves 4

4 fl oz/120 ml vegetable oil
1 medium onion, finely chopped
1 lb/450 g small, young okra
3 green (under-ripe) bananas
½ lb/225 g tomatoes, peeled and chopped
3 tablespoons lemon juice
2 small fresh hot chilli peppers, preferably red
1 tablespoon fresh coriander, chopped
salt, freshly ground pepper
1 lb/450 g peeled, cooked prawns
freshly cooked brown rice

In a frying pan heat the oil and sauté the onion until it is soft. Trim the okra and cut into ½ inch/1 cm slices and add to the onion. Sauté the mixture for about 3 minutes. Peel the bananas and cut them into ½ inch/1 cm slices. Add to the frying pan with the tomatoes, the chilli peppers, seeded and chopped, the coriander and salt and pepper to taste. Simmer for 5 minutes or until the vegetables are tender. Add the prawns and simmer just long enough to heat them through. Serve on a warmed dish surrounded by the rice.

TUNA AND RED KIDNEY BEAN SALAD

Serves 2 to 3

½ lb/225 g red kidney beans
salt, freshly ground pepper
8 oz/225 g canned tuna fish
1 sweet green pepper, seeded and finely chopped
1 sweet red pepper, seeded and finely chopped
1 Spanish or Italian red onion, finely chopped
1 tablespoon lemon juice or wine vinegar
6 pitted black olives
6 pimento-stuffed green olives
1 tablespoon sweet paprika
4 tablespoons finely chopped parsley or fresh coriander, or a mixture

Wash and pick over the beans and put into a saucepan with cold water to cover. Bring to the boil over moderate heat, simmer for 5 minutes, remove from the heat and allow to stand, covered, for 1 hour. Drain and rinse and cover with fresh cold water. Bring to the boil, lower the heat and simmer until the beans are tender, about 1 hour. Add salt halfway through cooking. When the beans are cool, strain, reserving the liquid for soup. Chill lightly.

Drain the tuna, reserving the oil from the can. Flake the fish and put into a bowl. Add the sweet red and green peppers and the onion. Season with salt and freshly ground pepper. Add the lemon juice or vinegar to the reserved oil mixing well. Pour over the fish mixture, and toss to mix. Arrange the fish mixture in the centre of a serving platter. Surround with the beans. Sprinkle the fish with the paprika and scatter the black and green olives over it. Sprinkle the whole dish with the parsley. Serve with extra oil and vinegar, if liked.

STUFFED POTATOES WITH TUNA FISH

Mashed sardines can be used instead of tuna fish with equally good results.

Serves 4

> 4 large, even-sized baking potatoes well scrubbed, pricked lightly with a skewer and rubbed with oil
> yolks of 2 hardboiled eggs
> 3 tablespoons thick tomato purée
> 8 oz/225 g tuna fish in oil or sardines in oil
> salt, freshly ground pepper
> chopped parsley

Bake the potatoes in a preheated hot oven (450°F/230°C/gas 8) for 45 minutes, or until they feel soft when pressed. Remove from the oven and halve the potatoes. Scoop out the flesh and mash it smooth. Add the egg yolks, tomato purée and tuna fish, or sardines, mashed. Season to taste with salt and pepper. Fill the potato shells with the mixture. Warm through in a moderate oven (350°F/180°C/gas 4) for about 10 to 15 minutes. Sprinkle with parsley and serve as a first course.

CURRIED FISH WITH PEANUTS

Potatoes and peanuts both contribute fibre to this pleasantly spicy dish. Those who love a hot curry can add crumbled dried hot chilli peppers, or cayenne pepper or a dash of a hot pepper sauce.

Serves 6

       butter
       2 lb/1 kg fillets of cod, haddock, monkfish or any firm-fleshed non-oily fish
       2 tablespoons peanut oil
       2 medium onions, finely chopped
       2 cloves garlic, minced
       1 tablespoon curry powder
       ½ lb/225 g tomatoes, chopped
       6 oz/175 g roasted peanuts, ground
       8 fl oz/225 ml coconut milk (page 25)
       1½ lb/700 g freshly cooked potatoes cut into 1 inch/2.5 cm cubes
       salt, freshly ground pepper
       1 tablespoon lemon juice

Butter a frying pan large enough to hold the fish comfortably and add water barely to cover. Bring to a simmer, cover and cook over low heat until the fish is done 8 to 10 minutes. Uncover the pan and let the fish cool. When it is cool enough to handle cut the fish into 1-inch/2.5 cm pieces. Set aside. Reserve the liquid.

In a large frying pan heat the oil and sauté the onions until they are soft. Add the garlic and sauté for 1 minute longer. Stir in the curry powder and cook for 2 minutes longer. Add the tomatoes, ground peanuts and coconut milk and cook, stirring, over moderate heat until the mixture is thickened. Add the fish and potatoes, season with salt and pepper and continue cooking over low heat until the dish is heated through. Sprinkle the lemon juice over it and put into a deep, heated serving dish. Serve with a fruit chutney, or a spicy hot sauce.

Variation: Almonds or walnuts may be used instead of peanuts.

KEDGEREE

(Fish with Rice and Pine Kernels)

Kedgeree began life as a dish in India called khitcherie or khichari. It was adopted by the British and in that felicitous way that migrant dishes evolve, it has become something quite different from the original, but very appetizing. There are a great many versions of the dish, and a number of cooks insist that it can be made only with smoked haddock. This is a very flexible, fibre-rich version using brown rice and unsmoked fish, not classical at all.

Serves 2

> 2 oz/50 g butter
> 1 large onion, preferably Spanish
> 1 lb/450 g halibut or cod, cooked and flaked
> ½ recipe for cooked brown rice (page 65)
> 2 oz/60 g pine kernels
> 2 hardboiled eggs, chopped
> 1 fresh hot red chilli pepper, seeded and chopped
> salt, freshly ground pepper

Heat the butter in a large frying pan and sauté the onion until it is soft and golden. Add all the remaining ingredients and cook, covered, over very low heat until heated through, about 10 minutes. Pile into a warmed serving dish and serve garnished with chopped parsley, if liked. Mango chutney is very nice with this and it makes a wonderful late breakfast.

MAIZE MEAL OR CORNMEAL

Maize, the staple cereal of the Americas, was unknown in Europe until Columbus discovered the New World. It is increasingly popular fresh as corn-on-the-cob, as tinned sweet corn, and as whole frozen corn kernels. Maize meal, made from dried corn kernels and sometimes called cornmeal is high in fibre like all the cereals, and has the appetizing flavour of fresh corn. It makes a wonderful topping for sausages as a different sort of Toad-in-the-hole (page 37), or for leftover beef, lamb or chicken as a different sort of Shepherd's Pie. It is also used in the West Indian dish Coo-Coo (below). Health food shops, supermarkets and most grocers carry maize meal.

CORNMEAL WITH COCONUT MILK AND FISH

This is one of the family of dishes that is known as Coo-Coo in the West Indies. Infinite variations are played on the theme and all are tasty and unusual.

Serves 4

> 1½ pints/800 ml coconut milk
> 1 teaspoon salt, or to taste
> ½ lb/225 g white or yellow cornmeal
> 1 lb/450 g cooked cod, haddock, or similar fish, flaked
> 1 fresh hot red chilli pepper, seeded and chopped
> butter

To make coconut milk add warm water to creamed coconut (sold in blocks almost everywhere) to bring it to the right consistency. Pour the coconut milk into a saucepan with the salt and bring to the boil over moderate heat. Lower the heat and pour in the cornmeal in a thin, slow, steady stream, stirring constantly with a wooden spoon until the mixture is smooth and thick. Fold in the fish and the chilli pepper and cook just long enough, covered, to heat the mixture through. If liked top with a little butter.

PRAWNS WITH BROWN RICE

The nutty flavour of brown rice goes beautifully with prawns and peppers turning this into a very special dish. Wild rice can also be used, in which case follow package instructions for cooking the wild rice.

Serves 6

2 tablespoons olive oil
1 large onion, finely chopped
1 clove garlic, chopped
1 sweet red pepper, seeded and chopped
1 green pepper seeded and chopped
1 lb/450 g tomatoes, peeled and chopped
salt, freshly ground pepper
4 oz/100 g pitted black olives, halved
1 oz/450 g cooked, frozen prawns, thoroughly defrosted
1½ recipes brown rice (page 65)

Heat the oil in a heavy casserole or saucepan and sauté the onion, garlic and peppers until the vegetables are soft. Add the tomatoes and cook for 5 minutes longer, or until the mixture is well blended. Season to taste with salt and pepper. Stir in the olives and, at the last minute and just long enough to heat them through, the prawns. Serve on a bed of hot, freshly cooked brown rice.

Variation: Stir 2 oz/50 g finely chopped parsley or coriander into the rice just before serving.

FISH PIE WITH SWEET POTATO TOPPING

White sweet potatoes give this fish pie a pleasantly
different flavour. The sweet potatoes used are sometimes
called boniatos, and are available in markets selling tropical
vegetables and often in supermarkets. They have a brown
or pink skin and white flesh and should not be confused
with the yellow-fleshed sweet potato with the orange-
brown skin called the Louisiana yam. This is a very good
vegetable, but not suitable for this dish.

Serves 6

    2 lb/900 g sweet potatoes
    1 oz/25 g butter
    ¼ pint/150 ml milk, about

    For the sauce:
    1½ oz/40 g butter
    3 tablespoons wholemeal flour
    ¼ teaspoon salt, freshly ground white pepper
    1 pint/575 ml milk, or use half fish stock, half milk
    2 lb/900 g fillets of any non-oily white fish (cod, haddock,
        halibut) cut into small pieces

Boil the potatoes in their skins until tender, about 20
minutes. Drain, peel and mash with butter and milk until
they are smooth and light adding more butter or milk if
necessary. Cover and set aside.

To make the sauce, melt the butter in a medium-sized
saucepan and stir in the flour. Cook over very low heat,
stirring with a wooden spoon for 2 minutes. Do not let the
flour colour. Remove the pan from the heat and gradually
stir in the milk, or the milk and fish stock mixture. Season
with salt and pepper, return the pan to the heat and
simmer, stirring, for about 5 minutes. Set aside.

Butter a 2½ pint/1.4 litre soufflé dish or casserole.
Arrange the fish, uncooked, on the bottom of the dish and

spoon the sauce over it. Top with the potatoes and dot with butter. Bake in a preheated moderate oven (350°F/180°C/ gas 4) for 45 minutes or until the dish is bubbly and the top is lightly browned. Serve from the dish.

Variation: Add 2 oz/50 g grated cheese (Gruyère, Cheddar or Parmesan) to the finished sauce before spooning it over the fish.

Variation: Add 2 teaspoons curry powder, or more to taste, to the butter when making the sauce.

Variation: Sprinkle the pie with 2 oz/50 g grated Parmesan and dot generously with butter before baking.

Meat and Poultry

CASSOULET

Languedoc's most famous dish, cassoulet, honours the white haricot bean. A hearty dish, it is splendid for entertaining friends and family at a Sunday lunch, for example.

Serves 6 to 8

> 1 lb/450 g white haricot beans
> bouquet garni: 2 or 3 sprigs parsley, bay leaf and sprig or
> ½ teaspoon of thyme, tied in a square of cheesecloth
> 1 lb/450 g pork skin, cut into strips and tied in a bundle
> with kitchen string
> 1 onion stuck with 2 cloves
> 2 cloves garlic, left whole
> salt, freshly ground pepper
> 2 tablespoons olive oil, or goose fat
> 2 lb/900 g lean, boneless pork cut into 2 inch/5 cm cubes
> 1 onion, finely chopped
> 2 cloves garlic, chopped

½ lb/225 g tomatoes, peeled, seeded and chopped
½ lb/225 g fresh pork sausages, coarse texture if possible
½ lb/225 g pork garlic sausage
2 oz/50 g freshly made breadcrumbs

Wash and pick over the beans and put them into a large saucepan with cold water to cover. Bring to the boil and cook, covered, for 2 minutes. Let them stand for 1 hour. Drain, and return them to the saucepan. Add the bouquet garni, the pork skin, the onion stuck with cloves, the whole garlic cloves, salt and pepper to taste and cold water to cover. Simmer, covered, for about 1 hour, or until the beans are tender. Drain the beans through a colander. Reserve the beans and the liquid and the pork skin. Discard the onion, garlic and bouquet garni.

In a large, heavy frying pan heat the oil or fat and sauté the pork cubes until lightly browned all over. Lift out the pork with a slotted spoon to a large casserole. Sauté the onion in the oil remaining in the pan. Add the onion to the casserole with the garlic and tomatoes and enough chicken stock or water barely to cover. Season with salt and pepper, cover and simmer for 30 minutes. In fat remaining in the frying pan brown the two types of sausage. When the casserole has been simmering for 30 minutes, add the sausages and cook for 30 minutes longer, or until the pork is tender. Lift out the meats, and cut the sausages into 1 inch/2.5 cm slices. Add the liquid to the reserved liquid from the beans.

To assemble the dish for its final cooking, cut the pork skin into squares and put them on the bottom of a large, deep earthenware or other type of casserole. Add one third of the beans and top them with half the meats, then another layer of one third of the beans, the remaining meats and the beans. Add the reserved cooking liquids and spread with half the breadcrumbs. Bake in a preheated, moderate oven (350°F/180°C/gas 4) for 45 minutes. Push the crust of breadcrumbs into the beans and top it with the

remaining crumbs. Bake for 45 minutes longer. Serve
direct from the casserole.

FEIJOADA COMPLETA

Feijoada could be described as the Brazilian version of
Cassoulet. It makes a magnificent high-fibre party dish. It
takes quite a lot of time, but not a great deal of work. If
exact ingredients are not available, use substitutes as
indicated.

Serves 8 to 10

> 1 lb/450 g dried beef, or use salt beef
> 3 lb/1.4 kg smoked ox tongue, or use fresh tongue
> 1 lb/450 g linguiça sausage, or use Spanish longaniza, or
>   any garlic sausage
> ½ lb/225 g lean bacon in one piece
> 1 lb/450 g pork sausages
> 1½ lb/700 g black kidney beans
> 1 lb/450 g beef chuck in one piece
> 2 tablespoons lard, or vegetable oil
> 2 medium onions, finely chopped
> 2 cloves garlic minced
> 1 lb/450 g tomatoes peeled and chopped
> 1 hot red chilli pepper, seeded and chopped or ¼ teaspoon
> hot pepper sauce, such as Tabasco

Soak the dried or salt beef overnight in a bowl of water. Put
it into a saucepan with water to cover and simmer 30
minutes. Drain. Set aside. In another saucepan simmer the
tongue for about 2½ hours. Cool in the cooking water
until it can be handled then remove the skin and any bone
and gristle. Put the linguiça or other sausage in a saucepan
with the bacon and cold water to cover and simmer for 15
minutes. Add the fresh pork sausages and simmer 15
minutes more. Drain and set aside.

Wash and pick over the beans and put them into a large saucepan with cold water to cover and simmer, covered, for 2 hours, adding hot water if needed as the beans absorb the water. Add all the meats that have been cooked together with the piece of beef chuck and simmer for 1 hour longer or until the meats and beans are tender.

In a frying pan heat the oil and sauté the onions until they are soft. Add the garlic and the tomatoes, the hot pepper or Tabasco, and salt and pepper to taste and simmer until the mixture is well blended. Add a ladleful of the beans and mash into the sauce. Cook until thick. Lift the meats out of the beans on to a platter. Stir the sauce into the beans and continue to cook over low heat. Slice the meats and arrange them on a large platter, or use two platters. Traditionally the tongue is put in the centre of a platter. The beans should be very soft, almost disintegrating into a sauce. Pour the beans into a large soup tureen.

Serve the *feijoada* with plain rice, cooked kale, a bowl of manoic (cassava meal) toasted in a frying pan with a little butter (8 oz/225 g cassava to 2 oz/50 g butter) for 2-3 minutes, 4 oranges, peeled and sliced and arranged on a serving dish and *Môlho de Pimenta e Limão* (Chilli Pepper and Lemon Sauce) made by mashing together 3 or 4 hot chilli peppers, 1 grated onion, 4 fl oz/125 ml lime or lemon juice, clove garlic, and salt. Use a blender or food processor or crush in a mortar with a pestle.

To serve the Feijoada, all the foods are put on to a table in suitable dishes and guests serve something of everything on to their plates, returning to the table for more when necessary.

BRAISED LEG OF LAMB WITH FLAGEOLETS

Lamb cooked in this way is exquisitely tender and the beans add a fibre bonus as well as adding a flavourful accompaniment. White haricot beans can be used instead of flageolets if these are hard to get.

Serves 6 to 8

>1 lb/450 g flageolets, or white haricot beans
>salt
>1 tablespoon vegetable oil
>4 lb/1.8 kg leg of lamb
>freshly ground pepper
>sprig rosemary
>2 large cloves garlic, chopped
>1 lb/450 g tomatoes, chopped or use 1 lb/450 g tinned
>   Italian plum tomatoes with the juice
>beef or chicken stock

Rinse and pick over the beans and put into a large saucepan with cold water to cover generously. Bring to a boil over moderate heat and simmer for 5 minutes. Remove from the heat and stand for 1 hour. Drain, add fresh water and salt to taste and simmer for 1 hour or until the beans are barely tender.

In a large casserole into which the lamb will fit comfortably, preferably oval in shape, heat the oil. Season the lamb with salt and pepper and brown it in the oil on all sides. In the last 2 minutes add the garlic. Add the tomatoes. If using tinned tomatoes, chop them coarsely. Add enough stock to come ⅔ of the way up the meat. Lay the sprig of rosemary on top of the lamb. Bring the liquid to the boil on top of the stove. Cover the casserole with aluminium foil and the lid and bake in a preheated moderate oven (350°F/180°C/gas 4) for 1½ hours. Remove the casserole from the oven. Strain, and add the beans. Cover and return to the oven and braise for 1½ hours longer or until the lamb is tender.

Lift the lamb out on to a platter and carve it into slices. Lift out the beans with a slotted spoon and put them round the meat. Moisten with a little of the cooking liquid. Skim

off any fat from the liquid and pour it into a gravy boat.
Serve with the lamb.

CHICKPEAS WITH TRIPE

Chickpeas have been appreciated for centuries as they are
one of the oldest foods known to civilization. High in
vegetable protein, rich in fibre, they are also very adaptable
and can change a dull dish into an interesting one.

Serves 6

> 3 lb/1.4 kg tripe cut into 2 inch/5 cm squares
> 3 tablespoons vegetable oil
> 2 medium onions, thickly sliced
> 2 cloves garlic, chopped
> 1½ lb/700 g potatoes, peeled and thickly sliced
> 1 lb/450 g tomatoes, chopped
> 1 lb/450 g cooked chickpeas (½ lb/225 g raw, about)
> 1 bay leaf
> ½ teaspoon thyme
> ½ teaspoon marjoram
> salt, freshly ground pepper

Chickpeas need a lot of cooking. The best method is to
wash them thoroughly and put them into a saucepan with
water to cover. Bring them to the boil over moderate heat
and let them boil for 5 minutes. Remove them from the
heat and let them stand for 1 hour. Then drain the
chickpeas, cover with fresh cold water and simmer until
tender about 1 hour longer.

Tinned chickpeas are available in most grocery shops. A
1 lb/450 g tin of cooked chickpeas is the equivalent of ½
lb/225 g raw chickpeas. They are very satisfactory and do
not go mushy which some other beans have a tendency to
do when tinned. It is an odd advantage of chickpeas that it is
almost impossible to overcook them.

Nibble a little of the tripe to see how much cooking it needs as tripe varies a great deal and often needs no separate cooking. If the tripe needs cooking, put it into a saucepan with cold water to cover and simmer until it is almost tender. Drain and reserve the liquid. Heat the oil in a frying pan and sauté the onions until they are golden. Add the garlic and sauté for 1 or 2 minutes longer. Lift out the onions and garlic with a slotted spoon and add to the tripe. In the oil remaining in the frying pan, adding a little more if necessary, sauté the potatoes until they are golden brown. Add them to the tripe with the tomatoes and chickpeas and the seasonings. Add enough of the reserved liquid barely to cover the mixture and simmer, covered, until the potatoes are tender, about 20 minutes.

CHICKEN IN PEANUT SAUCE

Peanuts have a lot of fibre making this deliciously different chicken dish good for one as well.

Serves 4

>2 tablespoons peanut oil
>3 lb/1.4 kg chicken, cut into serving pieces
>2 medium onions, finely chopped
>¾ pint/450 ml chicken stock
>6 oz/175 g peanuts, dry roasted if possible, and finely ground
>¼ teaspoon nutmeg
>½ teaspoon cayenne pepper
>salt, freshly ground pepper

Heat the oil in a frying pan and sauté the chicken pieces until they are golden all over. Transfer them to a flameproof casserole. In the oil left in the pan, adding a little more if necessary, sauté the onion until it is soft. Add it to the casserole.

Pour the chicken stock into the frying pan. Stir in the ground peanuts, nutmeg and cayenne, and salt and pepper to taste. Bring to the boil and simmer, stirring for 2 or 3 minutes or until the mixture is smooth. Pour it over the chicken. Cover and simmer until the chicken is tender, about 35 to 40 minutes. Serve the chicken on a bed of brown rice accompanied by side dishes of sliced green peppers, sliced bananas, cucumber sticks, mango chutney, sliced tomatoes and hot pepper sauce.

RABBIT AND PEANUT RAGOÛT

For anyone seeking a low fat meat, rabbit is the answer. It is lean and flavourful and lends itself to all sorts of cooking techniques. This one is simplicity itself, and is wonderfully tasty.

Serves 4

1½ oz/15 g butter
2 oz/50 g salt pork, cut into dice
2½ lb/1 kg rabbit, cut into serving pieces
salt, freshly ground pepper
2 tablespoons plain flour
1 medium onion, finely chopped
1 sweet green pepper, seeded and finely chopped
2 sweet red peppers, seeded and finely chopped
1 clove garlic, crushed
6 oz/175 g roasted peanuts, ground
salt, freshly ground pepper
¾ pint/400 ml beef stock

Heat the butter in a heavy frying pan and sauté the salt pork until it is crisp and browned. Transfer the pieces with a slotted spoon to a casserole. Season the rabbit pieces with salt and pepper and dredge with the flour, shaking to remove the excess. Brown them, in batches, in the fat remaining in the frying pan, adding more if necessary. Transfer them to the casserole. Add the onion, peppers and garlic to the frying pan and sauté them until the onion is soft. Add to the casserole with the peanuts, salt and pepper to taste and beef stock, stirring gently to mix. Bring to a simmer, cover and cook over low heat for about 1½ hours, or until the rabbit is tender. Serve with brown rice, or whole wheat spaghetti, or brown lentils.

TOAD-IN-THE-HOLE
(Sausages in Batter)

This old favourite can be turned into a high-fibre meal by using wholemeal instead of white flour, and serving a fresh tomato or a sweet red pepper sauce with it.

Serves 4

> 2 tablespoons dripping, lard or vegetable oil
> 1 lb/450 g pork sausages
> 4 oz/100 g wholemeal flour
> 1 teaspoon cream of tartar
> ½ teaspoon bicarbonate of soda
> 1 teaspoon salt
> 2 large eggs
> 4 fl oz/125 ml milk
> 4 fl oz/125 ml water

Preheat the oven to 425°F/220°C/gas 7. Put the fat into 9 by 5 inch/23 by 12.5 cm baking tin, and heat it in the oven Arrange the sausages in the baking tin and return it to the oven to lightly brown the sausages, about 5 minutes.

Meanwhile sift the flour, cream of tartar, bicarbonate of soda and salt into a large bowl. Make a well in the centre and break the eggs into the well. Start to mix the eggs into the flour, gradually adding the milk and water to make a smooth batter. This can be done in a food processor. Combine the dry ingredients in the food processor, mix the eggs with the milk and water, start the machine and pour the liquid mixture gradually in through the feed tube until the batter is smooth, about 30 seconds.

As soon as the sausages have browned lightly and the fat is very hot, lift out the baking tin and quickly pour the batter over the sausages. Return the tin to the oven and bake until the batter is puffed and browned and a knife inserted in the centre comes out clean.

Serve with fresh tomato sauce, or sweet red pepper sauce and a green vegetable or a salad.

SAUSAGES WITH CORNMEAL TOPPING

Serves 4

> butter
> 1 lb/450 g pork sausages
> 1 pint/575 ml milk
> 8 oz/225 g maize meal, preferably stone ground
> 1 oz/25 g butter, cut into bits
> 1 teaspoon salt
> 1½ teaspoons baking powder
> 3 large eggs, well beaten

Butter a 2½ pint/1.4 litre baking dish. Prick the sausages and arrange them in the dish. Pour the milk into a medium-sized saucepan and heat it to scalding point (when bubbles form round the edges of the pan). Stirring constantly with a wooden spoon to prevent lumps forming, pour in the maize meal in a slow thin steady stream. Remove the saucepan from the heat and beat in the butter, bit by bit. Stir in the salt. Stir the baking powder into the eggs and stir them into the maize mixture. Pour the batter over the sausages and bake in a preheated, moderate oven (375°F/190°F/gas 5) for about 45 minutes or until a knife inserted into the centre comes out clean. Serve from the baking dish, with Sweet Red Pepper Sauce or Fresh Tomato Sauce (pages 99–100).

BEEF AND CORNMEAL PIE

Serves 4 to 6

    2 tablespoons vegetable oil
    2 medium onions, finely chopped
    2 cloves garlic, minced
    1 lb/450 g lean minced beef
    1 lb/450 g tomatoes, peeled and chopped
    1 lb/450 g whole kernel sweetcorn, tinned or frozen
    3 oz/75 g sliced black olives
    4 oz/125 g cornmeal
    1 teaspoon salt
    2 teaspoons chilli powder
    salt, freshly ground pepper
    2 eggs, lightly beaten
    8 fl oz/225 ml milk

In a large, heavy frying pan heat the oil and sauté the onions until they are soft. Add the garlic and the beef and cook, breaking up the beef with a fork, until the meat is lightly browned. Add all the remaining ingredients, mixing thoroughly. Turn the mixture into a greased baking dish, (about 12 × 7 × 2 inches/30 × 18 × 5 cms) and bake in a preheated moderate oven (350°F/180°C/gas 4), until the top is lightly browned and a knife inserted in the centre comes out clean. Serve with fresh tomato sauce or sweet red pepper sauce and a green vegetable or a salad.

Vegetables

JULIENNE OF LEEKS AND CARROTS

This is a delicious vegetable combination which goes beautifully with grilled lamb chops. It is also good with poultry and grilled fish.

Serves 4

> 1 lb/450 g leeks, white part only
> 1 lb/450 g young carrots
> Salt, Freshly ground pepper
> 2 oz/50 g butter

Use the green part of the leeks when making stock, especially for soups. Wash the leeks very thoroughly and trim the root end. Cut into julienne (thin, matchlike strips). Put into a bowl.

Wash and scrape the carrots and trim the ends. Cut into julienne the same size as the leek strips. Add to the leeks. Season with salt and generously with pepper. Butter a flameproof baking dish, add the leek and carrot mixture, dot with the butter, cover with aluminium foil and cook over very low heat for about 20 minutes or until the vegetables are tender. If the vegetables are young and fresh they will cook in their own juices. If necessary add a little water.

SAUTÉED LEEKS

Serves 6

> 2 lb/900 g leeks, trimmed and thoroughly washed
> 2 oz/50 g butter
> water or stock if necessary
> salt, freshly ground pepper

Choose young, juicy leeks and discard almost all the green part. Chop the vegetables coarsely. Heat the butter in a large, heavy frying pan. Add the leeks, stir to mix. If necessary add a little water or stock. Season with salt and pepper, cover and cook until the leeks are tender, about 10 minutes.

GREEN BEANS WITH WATER CHESTNUTS

The crunchy texture and delicately nutty flavour of the water chestnuts are delicious with fresh green beans. Frozen whole green beans can be used if care is taken not to over cook them. They should be tender, but still crisp.

Serves 6

> 2 lb/900 g green beans, topped, tailed and halved
> salt
> 2 tablespoons vegetable oil
> 4 oz/100 g water chestnuts, sliced

Bring a large saucepan of salted water to the boil. Add the beans, bring the water back to the boil over high heat, lower the heat to moderate and simmer the beans, uncovered, for 8 minutes or until tender but still crisp. Drain and transfer to a vegetable dish. Toss with the oil and water chestnuts.

Variation: Omit the oil and water chestnuts. Toss the cooked beans with 1 oz/30 g butter then toss again with 4 oz/100 g sliced raw mushrooms.

SALSIFY AND SCORZONERA

These are both root vegetables belonging to the daisy family. Salsify is better known as oyster plant. Its near relative scorzonera has a black skin, and as far as I know has no common name in English. The roots discolour on contact with the air, so should be peeled or scraped under cold running water and dropped into a bowl of water acidulated with vinegar or lemon juice.

Serves 6

> 1 lb/450 g salsify, scraped and cut into 1 inch/2.5 cm pieces
> 1 lb/450 g scorzonera, scraped and cut into 1 inch/2.5 cm pieces
> 1 tablespoon lemon juice or vinegar
> salt
> butter or margarine

Drop the vegetables into a large saucepan full of boiling salted water with the vinegar or lemon juice added. Simmer, covered, until the vegetables are tender, about 10 to 15 minutes. Drain and transfer to a vegetable dish with a little butter or margarine. Serve instead of rice or potatoes.

Variation: Scrape ½ lb/225 g carrots, slice and add to the vegetables when cooking. The orange colour is very pretty with the pale salsify and scorzonera.

SPINACH WITH NEW POTATOES

This simple vegetable dish can be varied to provide exciting new combinations of flavours. It is also high in fibre.

Serves 6

    2 lb/1 kg spinach
    1 lb/450 g new potatoes
    1 tablespoon vegetable oil
    2 cloves garlic, chopped
    salt, freshly ground pepper
    large pinch freshly ground nutmeg, or ground coriander
       seed, or ground cardamom

Clean and trim the spinach and discard any wilted leaves. Drop the spinach into a very large saucepan of briskly boiling salted water. Bring back to the boil over high heat and cook, uncovered, for 4 minutes. Drain in a colander then plunge immediately into cold water. Drain. Using the hands, squeeze out as much of the water as possible then lay the spinach along the edge of a bamboo mat, or place it in a tea towel. Roll up the mat or cloth and squeeze out the water. Chop and set aside.

Scrub the potatoes thoroughly, then chop them coarsely. Put them into a saucepan with cold, salted water to cover, bring to the boil over high heat and simmer, covered, until they are tender, about 10 minutes. Drain and set aside.

In a heavy casserole or saucepan heat the oil and sauté the garlic for a minute or two. Add the spinach and the potatoes to the casserole. Season with salt, pepper and whichever spice is being used. Mix gently and cook just long enough to heat through. Serve with any plainly cooked fish, poultry or meat, or topped with fried or poached eggs as a main course.

Variation: Instead of the potatoes use cubed parsnips, sweet potato, or celery root (celeriac). Instead of spinach use green beans or fennel.

SPINACH WITH WALNUTS

Serves 4 to 6

> 2 lb/900 g spinach
> salt
> 2 tablespoons vegetable oil, or butter
> 2 oz/60 g walnuts, coarsely chopped

Wash and trim the spinach. Drop the spinach into a large saucepan full of briskly boiling salted water, bring back to the boil and boil for 4 minutes. Drain and plunge the spinach into cold water. Drain thoroughly and squeeze out all the water. An easy way to do this is to lay the spinach on a bamboo mat or on a tea towel, roll up and squeeze gently to press out the moisture. Chop the spinach. In a frying pan heat the oil or butter add the walnuts, sauté for 1 or 2 minutes, then add the spinach and heat through, stirring to mix the spinach and walnuts.

Variation: Omit the walnuts. Instead sauté 4 oz/100 g mushrooms, sliced, in the oil or butter and toss them with the spinach.

Variation: Broccoli is an attractive vegetable with a useful amount of fibre. It can be cooked with walnuts or with mushrooms in the same way as spinach.

Trim the broccoli stems. Bring a large saucepan of salted water to the boil, drop in the broccoli and simmer for 5 minutes. Test the stems with a paring knife to see if they are tender, if not, cook for another minute or two. Drain and toss with the sautéed walnuts or mushrooms.

BRUSSELS SPROUTS WITH CHESTNUTS

Both Brussels sprouts and chestnuts are delicious by themselves but together they can transform a plain meal into a very special one.

Serves 6

> 1½ lb/675 g Brussels sprouts, washed and trimmed
> salt
> 1½ oz/45 g butter
> 1 lb/450 g tin whole cooked chestnuts, rinsed and drained
> freshly ground pepper
> ⅛ teaspoon freshly ground nutmeg

Bring a large saucepan of salted water to the boil. Add the Brussels sprouts, bring the water back to the boil over high heat, lower the heat to moderate and simmer the sprouts, uncovered, for 8 minutes, or until tender but not soggy. Drain and set aside. Heat the butter in the saucepan, add the sprouts and the chestnuts, season with pepper and nutmeg and heat through, shaking the pan from time to time for about 2 minutes.

BOILED GREEN BANANAS

Green (unripe) bananas are often available at the greengrocer's and always in Asian and West Indian shops and markets. They make a pleasant change as a starchy vegetable to accompany a main course and add fibre to the day's food.

Serves 6

> 6 medium sized green bananas, peeled
> salt

Put the bananas into a saucepan large enough to hold them

comfortably. Pour in enough water to cover, add salt, bring
to the boil, lower the heat and simmer, covered, for 15
minutes or until the bananas are tender. Drain and serve
with a little butter or sauce such as tomato or sweet pepper.

GREEN PEA AND FENNEL PURÉE

Serves 6 to 8

Most vegetables are high in fibre but it is easy to get tired of
eating the same vegetables with meal after meal. Combin-
ing vegetables in new ways refreshes the palate. This is an
unexpected and brilliant combination.

> 2 lb/900 g fennel bulbs
> 1 oz/30 g unsalted butter
> Salt, freshly ground black pepper
> large pinch grated nutmeg
> 1 lb/450 g frozen peas thoroughly defrosted, or cooked,
> fresh peas if available

Cut off and discard the tops of the fennel down to the
bulbs, or keep the tops for use in soups or sauces. Trim
away any tough or discoloured sections. Cut the fennel
into thin, lengthwise slices. Have ready a large saucepan
filled with briskly boiling salted water. Add the fennel,
bring back to the boil and simmer, uncovered until it is
tender, about 10 to 15 minutes. Drain and purée in a
blender or food processor with the butter, salt, pepper and
nutmeg. Add the peas and process for a minute or so longer
until the purée is smooth. Keep warm until ready to serve.

YOUNG OKRA WITH CORNMEAL

This dish combines a green vegetable and starchy
vegetable and takes little time to make. It is very pleasant
with fish or any plainly cooked meat or poultry. Choose

okra that are only about 2 inches/5 cm long.

> 18 okras, about
> 2½ pints/1.4 litres water
> 1 teaspoon salt, or to taste
> ½ lb/225 g white or yellow cornmeal
> 2 oz/50 g butter

Rinse and trim the okras and cut them into thin slices. Bring the water to the boil in a medium-sized saucepan, add the salt and the okras and cook at a simmer, uncovered for 5 minutes. Pour the cornmeal into the okras in a thin, slow, steady stream, stirring with a wooden spoon over low heat then cook, stirring constantly, over moderate heat until the mixture is smooth and thick, about 5 minutes. Turn into a buttered vegetable dish and top with the butter.

If liked turn the cornmeal mixture into a buttered pudding basin then turn it out on to a serving platter and spread with the butter. It will retain its shape.

OKRA WITH AUBERGINE AND TOMATOES

This mixed vegetable dish is pleasant with any plainly cooked meat or poultry when served hot. Chilled lightly it makes an attractive salad for a first course.

Serves 4 to 6

> 1 lb/450 g aubergines peeled and cut into small cubes
> 4 fl oz/125 ml vegetable oil
> 1 medium onion, finely chopped
> 1 clove garlic, chopped
> 1 lb/450 g tomatoes, peeled and chopped
> 1 lb/450 g small young okra, rinsed and cut into ½ inch/1 cm slices
> 1 tablespoon chopped fresh coriander
> salt, freshly ground pepper

Heat the oil in a saucepan and sauté the onion until it is soft. Add the aubergine and garlic and sauté the mixture until the aubergine is lightly browned, stirring from time to time with a wooden spoon. Add the tomatoes and the okra and bring the mixture to a simmer. Simmer, covered for about 10 minutes, stirring occasionally. Season to taste with salt and pepper, add the coriander and cook, uncovered until the mixture is thickened, about 5 minutes. Serve hot.

If serving chilled sprinkle with a little more coriander.

OKRA WITH CORN AND TOMATO

All three vegetables are at their best in the market at the same time and combined they make a pleasant change from everyday vegetable choices.

Serves 4 to 6

> 2 oz/50 g butter
> 1 medium onion, finely chopped
> 1 sweet red or green pepper, seeded and chopped
> 1 lb/450 g small okra
> 1 lb/450 g tomatoes, peeled and chopped
> salt, freshly ground pepper
> 12 oz/350 g corn kernels

In a large frying pan heat the butter and sauté the onion with the pepper until the onion is soft. Add the okra, left whole, the tomatoes and salt and pepper to taste and simmer the mixture over moderate heat, stirring from time to time until the vegetables are tender, and the mixture well blended, about 15 minutes. Add the corn and simmer for 5 minutes longer. Serve hot.

CURRIED OKRA

Serves 4

2 oz/60 ml butter or vegetable oil
1 medium onion, finely chopped
1 tablespoon curry powder
8 fl oz/225 ml chicken stock
freshly ground pepper
1 lb/450 g young, small okra, trimmed
¼ pint/150 ml soured cream, or plain yoghurt

Heat half the butter or oil in a saucepan and sauté the onion until it is soft. Stir in the curry powder and sauté, stirring with a wooden spoon, for about 3 minutes. Stir in the chicken stock and season to taste with pepper. Set aside.

Heat the remaining butter or oil in a frying pan and sauté the okra until it is lightly browned. Add it to the saucepan with the curry mixture, bring to a simmer and cook, covered, over low heat until the okra is tender, 10 to 15 minutes. Stir in the soured cream or yoghurt and cook just long enough to heat through. Do not let the mixture boil as the yoghurt will curdle. Serve with grilled fish or hardboiled eggs.

STUFFED GREEN PEPPERS

Serves 6

6 medium-sized green peppers
1 recipe Refried Beans (page 00)
1 lb/450 g tomatoes, peeled and chopped
1 medium onion, chopped
1 clove garlic, chopped
8 fl oz/225 ml chicken stock, or water
salt, freshly ground pepper
2 eggs, separated
flour
lard or oil for frying

Impale the peppers, one by one, on a kitchen fork and toast over a gas or other flame until they are charred and blackened all over. Put the peppers into plastic bags or brown paper bags and leave to stand for 30 minutes. Take out and rinse off the charred skin under cold running water. Cut a slice off the stem end of the pepper to serve as a lid. Remove the seeds from inside. Stuff the pepper with the beans and replace the lid, securing it with toothpicks.

Combine the tomatoes, onion and garlic in a blender or food processor and reduce to a purée. Heat 1 tablespoon vegetable oil in a frying pan. Add the tomato purée and cook, stirring for 3 to 4 minutes. Add the stock and salt and pepper to taste and simmer for a minute or two to blend the flavours.

Beat the egg yolks in a bowl until thick. Beat the egg whites with a pinch of salt until they stand in peaks. Fold the whites into the yolks. Dip the prepared, stuffed peppers into flour, shaking to remove the excess. Heat about 2 inches/5 cm lard or oil in a large frying pan. Coat the peppers in the egg mixture and fry in the hot oil until golden brown all over. Heat the tomato sauce and add the peppers. Simmer, over moderate heat, just long enough to heat the peppers through, 2 to 3 minutes. Arrange the peppers on a warmed serving platter and pour the sauce over them.

Variation: Instead of beans, stuff the peppers with wedges of cheese such as mild cheddar, or Cheshire, or any similar cheese.

VEGETABLE MEDLEY

This is a first cousin to the Provençal *ratatouille*. It is a very flexible dish. Whatever is best at the greengrocer's can be chosen, or personal preference can be allowed to dictate the ingredients.

Serves 8

> 4 fl oz/125 ml olive oil, or vegetable oil if preferred
> 6 lb/2.7 kg vegetables including onions, courgettes, okra, sweet red and green peppers, aubergines, celery, celery root (celeriac), potatoes, fennel etc
> 1 lb/450 g tomatoes, peeled and chopped
> 2 cloves garlic
> salt, freshly ground pepper
> a herb bouquet including any of the following: mint, parsley, thyme, oregano, bay leaf, lovage, coriander, lemon balm, savory, according to taste
> black or green olives

Prepare the vegetables by cleaning and slicing. If using aubergines do not peel them; slice them and sprinkle with salt and put into a colander with a weight on top and leave for 30 minutes. Rinse and pat dry. Parboil the potatoes unpeeled, then peel and slice.

Heat the olive or vegetable oil in a large, heavy casserole. Add the onions and sauté until they are soft then add all the vegetables except the tomatoes and cook, covered, over low heat with the herbs and salt and pepper to taste for about 30 minutes or until the vegetables are tender but not mushy. Add the tomatoes and cook, uncovered, for 15 minutes longer.

Serve by itself or to accompany meat or poultry. Serve direct from the casserole.

VEGETABLE PLATTER

Vegetables do not have as much fibre as cereals, but they do have a useful amount and are certainly to be enjoyed. An attractive way for vegetable lovers to serve this favourite is to arrange the vegetables in rows or in circles on a large platter with sliced, ripe red tomatoes heaped in a pile in the centre. Black and green olives may be used as a garnish and a vinaigrette dressing or mayonnaise served separately. The vegetables may be served at room temperature, or lightly chilled. Served with crusty bread and butter, this makes a wonderful first course.

> Choose from any of the following vegetables:
> green peas
> cooked, sliced beetroot
> sliced celery
> cooked, sliced asparagus
> sliced avocados
> cooked corn kernels
> green beans, cut into ½ inch/1 cm slices
> cooked carrots, sliced
> cooked potatoes, sliced
> cauliflower cooked and separated into flowerets
> broccoli flowerets, cooked
> courgettes, sliced
> sliced radishes
> and any other favourite vegetables, either cooked or raw

BAKED POTATOES

Stuffed baked potatoes can make most satisfying lunch or supper dishes with, of course, the bonus of being fibre-rich. Complete the meal with a simple green salad, and fruit for dessert, or perhaps a little cheese. Choose large, even-sized baking potatoes.

> 6 potatoes, well scrubbed, dried, rubbed lightly with oil, and pricked in 5 or 6 places with a skewer

Put the potatoes on a baking sheet and bake in a preheated hot oven (450°F/230°C/gas 8) for 45 minutes, or until the potatoes feel soft when pressed. Halve the potatoes and scoop out the pulp. Mash it with 1 oz/30 g butter and a little milk until the potato is light and fluffy. Then mix it with an equal amount of cooked, puréed carrot, pumpkin, swede, parsnips, celeriac (celery root), spinach, cauliflower, green beans, beetroot, aubergine, broccoli, Jerusalem artichoke, kohlrabi, salsify, scorzonera, or any other vegetable. Season to taste with salt and freshly ground pepper and pile the mixture back into the potato shells. Sprinkle with grated cheese such as Parmesan, Gruyère, Cheddar, dot with butter or margarine, and grill until browned lightly.

The vegetable purées to be added to the mashed potato may be seasoned to taste. A little nutmeg may be added to spinach and pumpkin, a litle dill to carrots, and so on, according to personal taste. A little cream, or sour cream may be added to the finished purée if liked.

Eat the whole potato, including the skin.

CAVIAR POTATOES

This makes a very glamorous dish. Quantities cannot be given exactly.

Serves 4

> 4 large even-sized baking potatoes, scrubbed thoroughly, pricked lightly with a skewer and rubbed with oil
> caviar, lumpfish, or salmon caviar
> butter
> salt, freshly ground pepper
> soured cream

Bake the potatoes in a preheated hot oven (450°F/230°C/ gas 8) for 45 minutes or until they feel soft when pressed. Remove from the oven and cut a cross in the top of each potato with a sharp knife. Squeeze the potato slightly to open and put in a dab of butter. Top with a spoonful of caviar and a spoonful of soured cream. Serve with bowls of caviar and soured cream, butter and salt and pepper for guests to add according to taste. Serve with a spoon and fork.

BAKED POTATOES WITH SORREL CHIFFONNADE

Serves 4

> 4 large, even-sized baking potatoes
> oil
> butter or margarine
> warm milk
> 6 oz/175 g sorrel chiffonnade made with butter (see below)
> salt, freshly ground pepper
> grated Parmesan or Gruyère cheese

Bake the potatoes in the usual way (page 52). Halve the potatoes and carefully scoop the flesh out into a bowl, leaving a firm shell. Keep the shells warm in the turned off oven. Mash the potato until smooth using a little butter or margarine and warm milk until the mixture is light and fluffy. Beat in the sorrel chiffonnade and season to taste with salt and pepper. Refill the shells, and heat through. If liked, sprinkle with a little grated Parmesan or Gruyère cheese and run under the grill to melt the cheese. Serve as a first course, as an accompaniment to meat or poultry, or as the main course of a light meal.

SORREL

Sorrel is easy to grow and is often available in green-groceries. It has a light, clean, slightly acid flavour and since it reduces itself to a purée when cooked is best used as a purée, usually referred to as Chiffonnade of Sorrel. In this form it can be frozen and used, out of season, as needed. To freeze, put up the sorrel in small quantities; one of the best ways is to freeze the purée in ice trays, then remove and pack the cubes in plastic bags.

The chiffonnade can be made with or without butter.

PLAIN CHIFFONNADE

1 lb/450 g sorrel leaves
4 fl oz/125 ml water

Wash the sorrel in cold water. Cut away the heavy centre rib from the leaves. Stack the leaves, roll them up and shred them finely. Do this in batches. Bring the water to the boil in a heavy saucepan and add the sorrel, a handful at a time, stirring after each addition, until all the leaves have been added. Allow to simmer until they have reduced to a purée, about 10 minutes. Stir from time to time to prevent them sticking. If they are watery drain through a sieve and store in a plastic container until ready to use. A tablespoon stirred into any vegetable soup, or stew with vegetables, will enliven it. Sorrel has a natural affinity for fish.

CHIFFONNADE WITH BUTTER

1 lb/450 g sorrel leaves
1½ oz/45 g butter

Prepare the sorrel as for plain chiffonnade. Heat the butter in a heavy saucepan and add the sorrel, a handful at a time, stirring after each addition with a wooden spoon until all the sorrel has been added. Let it cook over very low heat until it has reduced to a purée, about 10 minutes. Cool and store.

CURRIED POTATOES AND PEAS
Alu Mattar

Serves 4 to 6

2 oz/50 *ghee*, or clarified butter, or vegetable oil
1 tablespoon fenugreek

2 cloves garlic, finely chopped
1 medium onion, finely chopped
2 tablespoons curry powder
salt, freshly ground pepper
¼ teaspoon ground hot red pepper
1 lb/450 g potatoes, peeled and cut
into cubes
1 lb/450 g green peas, if frozen thoroughly
defrosted (about 2 lb/900 g unshelled)
½ pint/275 ml water
2 tablespoons finely chopped fresh coriander or parsley

Heat the ghee or oil in a heavy frying pan or saucepan and
add the fenugreek and garlic cloves. Sauté over moderate
heat, stirring with a wooden spoon for 1 minute. Add the
onion and sauté until it is soft. Add the curry powder, salt,
pepper and hot pepper and sauté, stirring for 2 minutes
longer. Add the potatoes and the peas, stir to mix, add the
water and bring to the boil over high heat. Cover and cook
over low heat until the potatoes are tender. If necessary,
add a little water during cooking. The finished dish should
be quite dry. Sprinkle with coriander or parsley and serve.

Beans, Rice and Grains

BEANS

Beans are among the earliest of cultivated foods going back to prehistoric times. Kidney beans were first cultivated in Mexico, lima beans (butter beans) in Peru, broad beans, chickpeas and peas in the Middle East, black-eyed peas and pigeon peas in Africa, and soyabeans in China. All beans (the family is legion) are legumes. All are high in protein and in fibre and without them the cuisines of many countries would be completely altered. They are very important in Mexico, the Caribbean and South America. Distinctive cooking methods have developed in these countries where beans are not just a staple food, but a favourite food as well.

POT BEANS
Frijoles de Olla

The midday meal – *comida* – in Mexico would not be considered complete without beans being served as a separate course following the main course, and before the dessert. They are served in small bowls with some of the thick, flavourful broth. They are eaten with a spoon, or scooped up with a piece of tortilla. A little hot sauce, or pickled hot chilli pepper is often added and sometimes a little crumbled white cheese. They require little attention when they are cooking and are rich in fibre. They are very versatile and will go with any plainly cooked poultry or meat, as a vegetable. Topped with an egg and sprinkled with cheese they make the main course of a meal. Beans cooked by this Mexican method are very creamy in texture.

Serves 6 to 8

> 1 lb/450 g red kidney, pink, pinto or black kidney beans
> 2 medium onions, finely chopped
> 2 cloves garlic, chopped
> 1 bay leaf
> 2 small fresh hot green chilli peppers, seeded and chopped, or 1 teaspoon dried hot red chilli peppers, crumbled
> 1 oz/30 ml lard, or vegetable oil
> salt
> ½ lb/225 g tomatoes, peeled, seeded and chopped

Wash the beans and pick them over. Put them into a large saucepan or earthenware casserole with cold water to cover and half of the onion and garlic, the bay leaf and the hot chilli peppers. Cover and bring to a simmer over moderate heat. When the beans begin to wrinkle, after about 15 minutes cooking, add half the lard or vegetable oil. The beans will absorb all the water. When this happens add enough hot water to cover, hot tap water will do. Keep adding hot water as required, just enough to cover the beans. When the beans are soft, almost done, add salt, about 2 teaspoons/10 ml, or to taste. It is impossible to give exact cooking times for beans as a lot depends on how fresh they are, but about 1½ hours is usual. After adding the salt cook for 30 minutes longer without adding any more hot water. There should not be a great deal of liquid when the beans are done.

Heat the remaining lard or oil in a small frying pan and sauté the rest of the onion and garlic until the onion is soft. Add the tomato and cook for 2–3 minutes longer. Add a ladleful of beans and mash into the mixture. Cook until the beans are a smooth paste. Stir this back into the bean pot and cook over low heat, uncovered, until the liquid is thickened. Stir from time to time to prevent the beans sticking.

REFRIED BEANS
Frijoles Refritos

There is some mystery about the name of these beans since they are not fried twice. There are many theories. It is probably a matter of euphony since *frijoles fritos* sounds ungraceful in Spanish. *Refriar* comes in handy as it is an obsolete form of the verb to cool and these are cooked beans, later fried and mashed to a paste. However they got their name, they are marvellous with fried eggs and a spicy tomato sauce for breakfast or lunch and splendid as an alternative vegetable to rice or potatoes. And wondrously high in fibre.

Serves 6 to 8

Cook the beans as for Pot Beans (Frijoles de Olla) but when mashing them use a large frying pan and add the beans spoonful by spoonful, mashing until all have been added to the pan. Add more lard or oil from time to time until the beans form a heavy creamy paste. Form them into a roll, sprinkle them with grated Parmesan, or similar cheese and serve with little triangles of crisply fried tortilla, or with corn chips or anything similar as a cocktail nibble. They can also be used to stuff peppers (page 49).

BEANS, STATE OF MEXICO-STYLE
Frijoles Estilo Mexicano

This does not mean beans as cooked all over Mexico as the Spanish name might imply. It means beans as cooked in the State of Mexico and the Federal District where Mexico City is located. Mostly beans are cooked pot style. This makes a pleasant variation.

Cook the beans as for Pot Beans (Frijoles de Olla) just to the point where the salt has been added and the beans have been simmered for 30 minutes longer.

Using a slotted spoon lift out all the beans into a large bowl. Transfer a ladleful of the beans into a smaller bowl and mash with a fork until they are smooth. Stir them into the liquid in the saucepan.

Heat 1 oz/30 ml lard of vegetable oil in a large frying pan and add all the remaining beans. Sauté the beans, stirring from time to time with a wooden spoon, over moderate heat until they are quite dry, about 5 minutes. Return them to the saucepan and heat them through.

VENEZUELAN BLACK BEANS
Caraotas Negras

Venezuelans love black kidney beans. They are part of the national dish, Pabellon Caraqueño (Steak with Rice, Black Beans and Plantains). Mashed, and served with corn bread as an appetizer or cocktail nibble, they are called humourously *caviar criollo*, creole caviar, a nice compliment.

Serves 6 to 8

> 1 lb/450 g black kidney beans
> 2 tablespoons olive oil
> 1 medium onion, finely chopped

1 sweet red pepper, seeded and chopped
3 cloves garlic, chopped
1 teaspoon ground cumin seed
salt

Wash and pick over the beans. Put them to soak for 4 hours in a large saucepan with cold water to cover by about 2 inches/5 cm. At the end of the time the beans will have absorbed some of the water. Pour in enough to cover the beans by about 1 inch/2.5 cm. Bring to the boil, cover, and cook at a simmer until the beans are tender, about 1½ to 2 hours. In a frying pan heat the oil and sauté the onion and pepper until the onion is soft. Add the garlic and cumin and sauté for 2 minutes longer. Stir the mixture into the beans, season to taste with salt and cook, partially covered over low heat for 30 minutes longer. The beans will be quite dry.

BLACK KIDNEY BEANS
Fejão Preto

Black kidney beans are as popular in Brazil as they are in Venezuela. They are cooked just a little differently.

Serves 6 to 8

1 lb/450 g black kidney beans
2 tablespoons bacon fat
1 large onion, grated
1 clove garlic, crushed
Salt, freshly ground pepper
chopped parsley

Rinse and pick over the beans. Put the beans into a large, heavy saucepan with cold water to cover by about 2 inches/5 cm and soak for about 4 hours. Add enough water to cover the beans by about 1 inch/2.5 cm, bring to the boil, cover and simmer over moderate heat until they are tender, 1½ to 2 hours.

In a small frying pan heat the bacon fat and sauté the onion until it is soft. Add the garlic and cook for 1 or 2 minutes longer. Add a ladleful of beans, with their liquid to the pan and cook, mashing the beans with a fork, over low heat until the mixture is smooth and thick. Stir the mixture into the saucepan with the beans, season to taste with salt and a generous amount of pepper and cook, uncovered, over low heat for 30 minutes longer, stirring from time to time. Garnish with chopped parsley.

DRIED HARICOT BEANS WITH CORN AND PUMPKIN
Serves 4 to 6

½ lb/225 g white haricot beans or cannellini beans
2 tablespoons vegetable oil
2 tablespoons sweet paprika
1 large onion, finely chopped
1 lb/225 g tomatoes, peeled and chopped
½ teaspoon oregano
salt, freshly ground pepper
1 lb/225 g pumpkin, peeled and cut into 1 inch/2.5 cm cubes
½ lb/225 g corn kernels, if frozen thoroughly defrosted

Wash and pick over the beans. Put them into a large saucepan with cold water to cover, bring to the boil over high heat and boil for 5 minutes. Let stand, off the heat, for 1 hour. Drain, rinse and put on to cook in fresh water over moderate heat for about 1 hour, or until tender. Drain the beans, set aside. Reserve the cooking liquid.

In a frying pan heat the oil and stir in the paprika over low heat with a wooden spoon. As soon as the oil and paprika are well mixed add the onion and sauté until the onion is soft. Add the tomatoes, oregano, salt and pepper and simmer, stirring from time to time, until the mixture is thick and well blended, about 15 minutes.

Add the pumpkin to the reserved cooking liquid from the beans, cover and simmer for 15 minutes. Drain, reserving the liquid. Stir together the cooked beans, the tomato mixture and the pumpkin. Taste for seasoning and simmer very gently for 10 minutes to blend the flavours. Add a little of the reserved liquid if the mixture seems at all dry. Add the corn and cook, stirring from time to time for 5 minutes, adding more liquid if necessary. There should be enough liquid for the pumpkin to disintegrate, making a sauce.

SOYABEANS WITH MUSHROOMS AND PEPPERS

Serves 6

> 1 lb/450 g soyabeans
> 3 tablespoons vegetable oil
> 2 medium onions, finely chopped
> 1 sweet green pepper, seeded and chopped
> ½ lb/225 g mushrooms, sliced
> 1 clove garlic, minced
> salt, freshly ground pepper
> chopped chives or parsley

Wash and pick over the beans and put into a saucepan with cold water to cover. Soak overnight. Drain and rinse the beans and cook in fresh cold water to cover for 3 to 4 hours or until they are tender. Drain the beans, and set aside.

In a frying pan heat the oil and sauté the onions and green pepper until the onion is soft. Add the mushrooms, garlic and salt and pepper to taste and sauté until the mushrooms are cooked, about 5 minutes. Add the vegetable mixture to the beans and heat through. Serve as a side dish with any plainly cooked meat or poultry, garnished with chopped chives or parsley.

BAKED BEANS

Boston baked beans with brown bread, a Saturday night tradition in that city, were the inspiration of the universal favourite, tinned baked beans. This is an easily made home version.

Serves 6

> 1 lb/450 g dried white haricot beans
> 1 lb/450 g piece boneless belly of pork, skin scored
> 1 small onion
> 2 oz/50 g treacle
> 2 tablespoons brown sugar
> ½ teaspoon dry mustard
> ½ teaspoon ground ginger
> 1 teaspoon salt

Wash and pick over the beans and put them into a saucepan with cold water to cover and leave to soak overnight. Drain, cover with fresh water and cook, covered, over moderate heat until the beans are tender, about 1½ hours. Drain the beans reserving the liquid. Put the beans into a 7 pint/4 litre casserole or bean pot. Bury the pork and the onion in the beans. Mix together the treacle, sugar, mustard, ginger and salt. Bring the reserved liquid to the boil and add the treacle mixture. Pour over the beans. Add more water if necessary to cover the beans. Cover tightly and bake in a preheated very slow oven 250°F/130°C/gas ½ for 6 hours. Remove the cover for the last 30 minutes to let the beans form a crust.

Variation: Add 1 lb/450 g tomatoes, peeled and chopped to the pot with the treacle mixture. Salt pork can be used instead of fresh pork and is in fact more traditional in the original Boston baked beans.

BROWN RICE

This has a nice nutty flavour and texture and has the added
merit of being rich in fibre unlike polished white rice. It
takes longer to cook than white rice, with less water.
Cooking times and the amount of water may vary slightly
with different brands of rice. Use this recipe as a guide.

Serves 4 to 6

> 12 oz/350 g brown rice
> 1¼ pints/700 ml water
> 1 teaspoon salt

Put the rice into a heavy saucepan with a tight-fitting lid.
Add the water and salt and stir to mix. Bring to the boil,
covered, over moderately high heat then reduce the heat to
as low as possible and cook for 45 minutes. Do not take the
lid off during the cooking period. When the rice is tender
and all the liquid absorbed, cover the rice with a folded tea
towel and the lid and let it stand until ready to use. It will
keep warm for about 15 minutes. If the rice is to be used
cold, take the lid off to let it cool and prevent condensed
moisture dripping into it.

PEANUT RICE

This makes a very attractive accompaniment to a curry.
The peanuts add to the crunchy quality of the brown rice.

Serves 4 to 6

> 12 oz/350 g brown rice
> 1¼ pints/700 ml chicken stock
> 1 teaspoon salt
> 1 tablespoon butter
> 6 oz/175 g roasted peanuts, coarsely chopped

Put the rice into a heavy saucepan with a tight-fitting lid and the chicken stock and salt. Stir to mix, bring to the boil over moderately high heat, reduce the heat to low, and cook for 45 minutes or until the rice is tender and all the liquid absorbed.

Heat the butter in a small frying pan and sauté the peanuts for 2 or 3 minutes. Stir them, with the butter, into the rice. Serve immediately.

RICE AND BEANS

Rice and beans have a natural affinity for each other. Since beans take rather a long time to cook, though need little attention, it is a good idea to put on an extra ½ lb/225 g when cooking them so as to have leftovers on hand for dishes like rice and beans. There are a great many versions of rice and beans, all of them fibre-rich, all of them delicious.

BLACK HARICOT BEANS AND RICE

Serves 4 to 6

> 2 tablespoons olive oil
> 1 medium onion, finely chopped
> 1 clove garlic, minced
> 1 medium sized sweet green pepper, seeded and finely chopped
> ½ lb/225 g tomatoes, peeled and chopped
> salt, freshly ground pepper
> 1 lb/450 g cooked black haricot beans
> ½ recipe brown rice cooked (page 65)

Heat the oil in a heavy casserole, add the onion, garlic, and green pepper and sauté until the onion is soft. Add the tomatoes, and cook, stirring from time to time until the mixture is well blended. Season to taste with salt and pepper. Add the beans, mixing well and heat through. Fold in the rice, cooking just long enough to heat through.

COCONUT RICE AND RED KIDNEY BEANS

Serves 4 to 6

> 1½ pints/850 ml coconut milk (page 25)
> 2 oz/50 g boiled ham, coarsely chopped chilli
> 1 or 2 fresh hot red or green peppers, seeded and chopped
> 2 cloves garlic, minced
> ½ lb/225 g tomatoes, peeled and chopped
> 1 tablespoon fresh coriander, or parsley, chopped
> salt
> 12 oz/350 g brown rice
> ½ oz/225 g cooked red kidney beans

Pour 4 fl oz/125 ml of the coconut milk into a heavy saucepan that has a tightly fitting lid. Add the ham, hot chilli peppers, garlic, tomatoes and coriander and salt to taste and simmer for 2 or 3 minutes. Stir in the rice and the rest of the coconut milk, then stir in the beans and cook, covered, over low heat until the rice is tender and all the liquid absorbed, about 20 minutes. Serve as a side dish or, topped with fried or poached eggs as a main course.

LENTIL PURÉE

Lentils make a fine substitute for potatoes, rice or noodles in any meal.

Serves 6

> 1 lb/450 g brown lentils
> 2 tablespoons butter or vegetable oil
> 1 medium onion, finely chopped
> 2 stalks celery, chopped
> ½ sweet red or green pepper, seeded and chopped
> 1 clove garlic, chopped
> ¼ lb/100 g tomatoes, chopped
> 1 bay leaf

½ teaspoon each thyme, marjoram and savory
salt, freshly ground pepper
butter (optional)

Wash and rinse the lentils and put them into a large saucepan with cold water to cover. Bring to the boil, covered, over moderate heat. Remove from the heat and stand, covered, for 1 hour. Drain, and set aside.

In a frying pan heat the butter or oil and sauté the onion, celery, sweet pepper, garlic and tomatoes until the onion is soft. Stir into the lentils. Add the bay leaf, thyme, marjoram, savory, salt and pepper and water barely to cover. Cover and simmer until the lentils are tender and quite dry, about 1 hour. If there seems to be a great deal of liquid, simmer partially covered for the last 15 minutes of cooking. The lentils should be reduced to a purée but with a good deal of texture. They should not be mushy. If liked stire in some butter when serving.

The lentils may be cooked in stock instead of water if preferred. Split peas may be cooked in the same way.

DAL

In India the legumes – lentils, dried peas and beans – are known as dal. They are a very good source of fibre and can be served as a side dish to accompany meat or poultry. They can also be the main course of a vegetarian meal.
Serves 4 to 6

1 lb/450 g brown lentils or green or yellow split peas
water
salt
2 oz/50 g butter
2 medium onions, finely chopped
½ teaspoon ground turmeric
½ teaspoon ground cumin
¼ teaspoon cayenne pepper
fresh coriander leaves, about 4 tablespoons

Put the lentils or split peas in a saucepan with water to cover and the salt, cover and cook until almost done. The quick cooking variety will be tender in about 20 minutes.

Heat the butter in a frying pan and sauté the onions until golden brown. Add the turmeric, cumin, and cayenne pepper and mix thoroughly, off the heat. Stir the mixture into the dal and simmer for 5 minutes longer, or until done. Stir in the fresh coriander leaves and serve.

PURÉED CHICKPEAS

Serve the chickpeas instead of rice, pasta or potatoes. It makes a pleasant change.

> 1 lb/450 g chickpeas cooked in the usual way (page 34)
> salt, freshly ground pepper
> 1 oz/30 g butter
> 2 cloves garlic, finely chopped (optional)
> 1 oz/30 g parsley, finely chopped
> grated lemon peel (optional)

Mash the cooked chickpeas while still hot, or purée in a food processor. Season with salt and pepper and beat in the butter. Transfer to a warmed vegetable dish and sprinkle with the garlic, parsley and a little grated lemon peel.

GRAINS

It is hard to understand why these grains are not more used as a substitute for rice and potatoes. They make a very attractive change. In the West Indies millet is often called guinea corn. Cracked wheat is often sold as bulgur, while kasha may be better known as buckwheat.

MILLET

Serves 6 to 8

> 14 oz/400 g millet
> 1 medium onion, finely chopped
> 1 teaspoon salt
> freshly ground pepper
> 1½ ounces/40 g butter

Toast the millet in a heavy frying pan, preferably iron until it is golden and has a nutty fragrance. Add the remaining ingredients and 1¼ pints/700 ml boiling water. Stir, bring back to the boil, lower the heat and cook, covered, until the millet is tender and all the liquid absorbed about 20 minutes. If necessary add a little more hot water from time to time and stir occasionally. Fluff with a fork and serve.

CRACKED WHEAT (BULGUR)

Serves 6 to 8

> 1½ oz/40 g butter
> 1 medium onion, finely chopped
> 12 oz/350 g cracked wheat
> salt, freshly ground pepper
> 1¼ pints/700 ml chicken stock

Heat the butter in a heavy frying pan and sauté the onion until it is soft. Add the cracked wheat, stirring to mix and cook over moderate heat for 2 or 3 minutes until the bulgur is slightly coloured. Like the millet it will have a nut-like fragrance. Season with salt and pepper and stir in the chicken stock. Bring to a simmer, cover and cook over low heat for 1 hour. Add more stock if necessary during the cooking time and stir occasionally. Water may be used instead of stock if preferred. Fluff with a fork before serving.

BARLEY AND MUSHROOM CASSEROLE

Serves 6

1 oz/30 g butter
1 small onion, finely chopped
2 large cloves garlic, finely chopped
8 oz/225 g mushrooms, sliced
8 oz/225 g pearl barley
1 small red pepper, seeded and cut into strips
3/4 pint/450 ml chicken stock
1/2 teaspoon ground coriander
salt, black pepper
chopped basil or parsley

Heat the butter in a heavy casserole and add the onion and garlic. Cook gently for 3–4 minutes, then turn up the heat and add the mushrooms. Cook, stirring occasionally, for about 3 minutes. Put in the barley and cook for 3–4 minutes, stirring all the time until the barley is golden. Add the red pepper, the stock and season with corriander, salt and pepper. Cover with a well-fitting lid, reduce the heat to a simmer and cook for about 30 minutes, or until the barley is tender and has absorbed all the liquid. Check from time to time for moisture; if necessary remove the lid to allow for evaporation, or if the barley is too dry, add a little more stock. Serve sprinkled with chopped basil or parsley.

Salads

WHOLEMEAL SPAGHETTI SALAD

This makes a delicious main course for a lunch or dinner
and is ideal for warm weather when appetites become
jaded. And the fibre content is gratifyingly high. This
recipe serves 2 generously. It can be doubled or trebled for
larger numbers.

> 6 oz/175 g wholemeal spaghetti
> salt
> ½ lb/225 g courgettes
> ½ medium-sized green pepper
> ½ medium-sized red pepper
> ½ lb/225 g tomatoes, peeled
> 1 Spanish or Italian red onion
> 4 oz/100 g carrot, scraped and grated
> 2 artichoke bottoms, cut in quarters
> 4 oz/100 g garlic sausage such as Bologna
> 6 pitted black olives
> 2 tablespoons each chopped parsley and fresh basil, or
>   chives or other herb in season
> freshly ground pepper

2 oz/50 g Provolone or similar cheese, coarsely grated

for the vinaigrette:
1 large clove garlic, crushed
3 tablespoons vegetable oil
1 tablespoon olive oil
1 tablespoon aceto balsamico (Italian vinegar) or wine
   vinegar or lemon juice

Put the spaghetti into a large saucepan full of briskly boiling heavily salted water and boil for 15 minutes. Drain in a colander and put into a large salad bowl.

Cut the courgettes and peppers into julienne (match stick pieces) and blanch in briskly boiling salted water for 1 or 2 minutes according to taste. Drain and chill. Chop the tomatoes into bite-size pieces. Halve the onion and slice very thinly. Cut the sausage into bite-size pieces. Combine with all the other ingredients except the cheese and the vinaigrette in a large salad bowl with the spaghetti.

In a small bowl combine the garlic, two types of oil, the vinegar, and salt and pepper to taste and beat with a fork to combine. Pour over the salad, and toss to mix. Sprinkle with the cheese.

FOUR BEAN SALAD

Endless variations can be played on the bean salad theme. Pale green flageolet, red or black kidney beans, white haricot or cannellini beans, or chickpeas are all suitable to be mixed together for this robust, appetizing, high fibre salad, together with fresh green beans and mushrooms. This is a version I like very much.

Serves 4

4 oz/100 g dried flageolets
4 oz/100 g cannellini beans

4 oz/100 g red kidney beans
1 medium onion, cut into thirds
3 whole cloves
3 cloves garlic
3 sprigs each thyme and parsley
3 sprigs celery with leaves, or 3 sprigs lovage
salt, freshly ground pepper
5 tablespoons vegetable oil
2 tablespoons lemon juice
8 oz/225 g green beans cut into 1 inch/2.5 cm pieces
2 oz/50 g fresh mushrooms, sliced

Put the dried beans into 3 separate saucepans with cold water to cover. Bring to the boil over moderate heat, boil for 2 minutes, turn off the heat and stand, covered, for 1 hour. Drain, cover with fresh water by about 2 inches/5 cms. Add ⅓ onion stuck with a clove, 1 clove garlic, a bouquet garni of thyme, parsley and celery or lovage tied with a piece of cotton, to each saucepan and simmer until tender, about 1 hour. Season with salt and pepper and simmer 5 minutes longer. Remove and discard the bouquet garni. Drain and reserve any liquid for making soup. Cool the beans slightly. Combine them in a wooden salad or glass salad bowl with the oil and lemon juice.

Meanwhile boil the green beans in salted water to cover until tender but still crisp, about 15 minutes if fresh, 8 minutes if frozen. Fold them into the beans. Add the mushrooms and toss to mix.

MIXED BEAN, RICE AND VEGETABLE SALAD

Novelist Dolores de Soto Palà created this dish for informal parties in the Majorcan house where she and her husband, the sculptor Joan Palà spend part of the summer. It can be served with side dishes of cold meats, sausages, cheese or what you will. It has the merit of being delicious as well as good for you, and is ideal for a hot weather buffet lunch or supper. Amounts can be doubled or trebled.

Serves 6 to 8

> ½ lb/225 g haricot or cannellini beans
> salt
> ½ lb/225 brown rice
> ½ lb/225 g frozen corn kernels, thoroughly defrosted
> 1 large onion, preferably Spanish
> 2 green peppers
> 2 red peppers
> 1 medium sized cucumber
> 2 small courgettes
> 1 lb/450 g tomatoes
> 6 eggs, hardboiled, peeled and chopped
> 2 tablespoons capers
> freshly ground pepper
> ½ teaspoon thyme, finely chopped
> ¼ teaspoon ground cardamon
> 2–3 tablespoons lemon juice
> 3–4 fl oz/100–125 ml olive oil

Wash and pick over the beans and put them into a large saucepan with water to cover by about 2 inches/5 cm. Bring to the boil over high heat and boil for 2 minutes. Turn off the heat and let the beans stand, covered, for 1 hour. Drain and rinse then put to cook in fresh cold water to cover for 1 hour, or until they are tender. About 15 minutes before the beans are ready, salt to taste. Drain and set aside until ready to use.

Put the rice into a heavy saucepan and rinse thoroughly until the water runs clear. Pour in ¾ pint/420 ml cold water and ½ teaspoon salt. Bring to the boil, covered and cook over the lowest possible heat until the rice is tender and all the liquid absorbed, about 20 minutes. Cover the rice with a folded tea cloth and the saucepan lid and leave until ready to use. Drop the corn kernels into boiling, salted water and simmer for 5 minutes. Drain and set aside until ready to use.

Peel the onion and chop finely. Do not peel the peppers, cucumber, courgettes or tomatoes. Remove the stems and seeds from the peppers. Chop all the vegetables finely and combine in a large salad bowl with the onion. Add the rice, beans and corn, eggs and capers. Season with salt, pepper, the thyme, cardamom and lemon juice. Pour the olive oil over the salad and toss lightly. Serve with side dishes of any meat, fish, sausages, poultry, and wholemeal bread.

BEAN SALAD

Serves 6

> 1 lb/ 450 g pink, pinto, brown or red kidney beans
> salt
> 4 fl oz/125 ml olive oil
> 1 clove garlic, crushed
> freshly ground pepper
> 1 tablespoon lemon juice
> 1 Spanish or red onion, thinly sliced
> 12 anchovy fillets, well drained
> 3 tablespoons capers, rinsed and dried
> 12–18 pitted black olives
> 1 lb/450 g peeled, sliced tomatoes
> 2 tablespoons fresh basil leaves, chopped

Wash and pick over the beans. Put into a saucepan with cold water to cover, bring to the boil and simmer for 2 minutes. Allow to stand for 1 hour. Drain, rinse and cover with fresh water. Simmer for 1 hour or until tender, adding salt in the last 15 minutes. Drain, and put into a salad bowl. While still hot, toss with a dressing made by beating together the olive oil, crushed garlic, salt, pepper and lemon juice. Serve the salad as a first course with each serving garnished with sliced onion, anchovy fillet, capers, and black olives. Arrange the tomatoes on the edge of the plates and sprinkle with the basil leaves. Drizzle with a little olive oil if liked.

SOYABEAN SALAD

Serves 6

1 lb/450 g soyabeans
½ lb/225 g mushrooms, sliced
18 Greek black olives, pitted
6 small tomatoes, quartered
6 spring onions, trimmed and sliced
1 green pepper, seeded and sliced
1 red pepper, seeded and sliced
3 fl oz/75 ml olive oil or vegetable oil
2 tablespoons lemon juice
1 clove garlic, crushed
salt and freshly ground pepper
4 oz/100 g low fat white cheese, such as fetta, cut into 1 inch/2.5 cm cubes (optional)

Wash and pick over the beans and put them into a saucepan with cold water to cover. Soak overnight. Drain and rinse the beans and cook in fresh cold water to cover for 3 to 4 hours or until they are tender. Drain the beans put them into a salad bowl.

Add the mushrooms, olives, tomatoes, spring onions and green and red peppers to the salad bowl. If liked blanch the peppers for 1 minute in boiling water, drain and cool. Mix together the olive or vegetable oil, lemon juice, garlic, and salt and pepper and pour over the salad. Toss lightly. If liked, garnish with the cheese.

MANGETOUT AND MUSHROOM SALAD

Serves 6

½ lb/225 g fresh mangetout/peas
½ lb/225 g mushrooms
1 red pepper
1 green pepper
½ lb/225 g small size tomatoes
3 tablespoons vegetable oil
1 tablespoon lemon juice
salt, freshly ground pepper

Top and tail the mangetout and remove any strings. Drop the peas into a large saucepan filled with briskly boiling salted water and blanch them for 1 minute. Drain and rinse under cold running water. Pat dry with paper towels and cut them in halves, crosswise on a diagonal. Put into a salad bowl.

Wipe the mushrooms with damp paper towels or a damp cloth to clean them. Trim the stems. Slice the mushrooms, and add to the mangetout.

Remove the stems and seeds from the peppers. Halve the peppers crosswise, then cut into thin strips. Quarter the tomatoes. Add them to the salad bowl.

Mix together the oil, lemon juice, salt and pepper. Pour it over the salad and toss lightly.

OKRA SALAD

Okra, especially the small ones increasingly available in greengroceries, make an interesting change from more usual vegetables. Choose okras 2–3 inches/5 cm–7.5 cm long.

Serves 4 to 6

1 lb/450 g okra
salt, freshly ground pepper

3 tablespoons vinegar, preferably rice vinegar
4 fl oz/125 ml vegetable oil

Rinse the okra in cold water then drop into a saucepan of briskly boiling salted water and cook for about 6 minutes, or until tender. Drain and allow to cool. Cut the okra into ½ inch/1 cm slices and put into a salad bowl. In a small bowl combine the vinegar, salt, pepper and oil, beating the mixture with a fork. Pour over the okra and toss lightly.

HERBED VEGETABLE SALAD

This is a lovely salad, stretching the cook's imagination to make substitutions and amendments. It provides an ideal setting for two people in a pleasant environment having this as all the lunch they'll need, except perhaps for a bottle of chilled white wine.

Serves 2 generously

6 oz/175 g wholemeal spaghetti
salt

for the vinaigrette:
4 tablespoons vegetable oil, or a mixture of vegetable and olive oil
1 tablespoon lemon juice, or cider or raspberry vinegar
1 teaspoon Dijon mustard
1 clove garlic, crushed
salt, freshly ground pepper

for the salad:
2 oz/50g parsley, preferably flat type, chopped
2 tablespoons chopped chives
1 oz/25 g chopped basil or fresh coriander
4 oz/100 g spring onion, chopped, using a little of the green part
1 tablespoon of any or all of the following fresh herbs, finely chopped: hyssop, mint, lemon balm, tarragon,

chervil, lovage
1 medium carrot, scraped and coarsely chopped
1 medium sized courgette, cut into julienne (match sticks)
4 oz/125 g green beans cut into ½ cm lengths
4 oz/125 g green peas, if frozen thoroughly defrosted
½ green pepper, seeded and cut into strips
½ red pepper, seeded and cut into strips

Put the spaghetti into a large saucepan full of well salted, briskly boiling water and boil for 15 minutes, or until tender but still firm to the bite. Drain in a colander and set aside.

Make the vinaigrette in a bowl. Mix all the ingredients together, beating with a small whisk or a fork until well blended.

If liked blanch the courgettes, green beans, peas, and green and red sweet peppers for 2 to 4 minutes in briskly boiling salted water. Drain and chill in the refrigerator briefly. Otherwise add them, uncooked, to the salad.

To assemble the salad put the spaghetti into a large salad bowl and pour the vinaigrette over it. Toss lightly. Add all the other ingredients and toss. Use the hands if it is more convenient.

For a more robust salad add ½ lb/225 g cooked chicken breast, shredded and ½ lb/225 g cooked prawns, coarsely chopped to the mixture when tossing.

ORIENTAL RICE SALAD

Serves 4 to 6

1 recipe brown rice (page 65)

for the vinaigrette:
4 tablespoons vegetable oil
1 tablespoon Japanese rice vinegar, or ponzu (citrus vinegar), or lemon juice

salt, freshly ground pepper

for the salad:
4 oz/100 g cooked, chopped prawns
4 oz/100 g cooked ham, chopped
4 oz/100 g cooked chicken breast, chopped
4 oz/100 g cooked squid, sliced (optional)
8 oz/225 g tofu (bean curd) cut into small cubes
8 oz/225 g bean sprouts
4 oz/100 g water chestnuts, sliced
4 oz/100 g bamboo shoots, sliced
4 oz/100 g celery, chopped
4 oz/100 g carrots, grated
½ red, ½ green pepper, seeded and chopped
4 oz/100 g courgettes, sliced
4 small tomatoes, quartered
1 tablespoon fresh coriander or parsley, chopped

Put the rice into a large salad bowl. In a small bowl beat together the ingredients for the vinaigrette and pour them over the rice. Toss well. Add all the remaining ingredients and mix thoroughly.

If liked blanch the sweet peppers and the courgettes for 4 minutes in boiling salted water, otherwise leave raw.

The amount of vinaigrette can be increased if liked.

CHICKPEA AND TOMATO SALAD

The crunchy chickpeas make this an unusual salad. Serve it as a main course for a light lunch or as a first course for a more elaborate dinner. Tinned chickpeas can be used if liked. Two 1 lb/450 g tins is about the equivalent of 1 lb/450 raw chickpeas.

Serves 6

3 tablespoons olive or vegetable oil
1 large Spanish onion, or 2 medium onions, finely chopped

1 lb/450 g raw chickpeas, cooked in the usual way (page 34)
1½ lb/700 g tomatoes, chopped
6 oz/175 g pitted black olives, halved
salt, freshly ground pepper
½ teaspoon ground coriander
2 oz/50 g parsley, finely chopped
tin anchovy fillets, drained, rinsed and patted dry

Heat the oil in a frying pan and sauté the onion until it is soft and golden. Stir in the cooked chickpeas and sauté for 2 or 3 minutes. Add the tomatoes and simmer, uncovered, until most of the liquid has evaporated. Add the olives and simmer 1 or 2 minutes longer. Season with salt, pepper and coriander. Stir in the parsley. Transfer to a serving dish. Arrange the anchovies in a decorative pattern on top of the salad and serve slightly chilled, or at room temperature.

WARM CHICKPEA AND APRICOT SALAD

This makes an unusual and appetizing first course.

Serves 4 to 6

2 oz/50 g dried apricots
½ lb/225 g chickpeas
3 tablespoons olive oil, or more to taste
salt, freshly ground pepper

Put the apricots to soak in warm water to cover for 30 minutes. Drain and chop coarsely. Cook the chickpeas in the usual way (page 34). Drain and while they are still hot toss with the olive oil. Add the apricots and season to taste with salt and pepper. Serve warm.

Variation: Lentils, cracked wheat (bulgur), or small white beans may also be used, instead of chickpeas. Pitted black olives may be added to the salad and chopped parsley or fresh coriander sprinkled on it as a garnish. The adventurous cook is invited to make additions.

MIXED VEGETABLE SALAD

Serves 8

½ lb/225 g Jerusalem artichokes, cooked and sliced
½ lb/225 g potatoes, cooked, peeled and cut into small dice
½ lb/225 g young carrots, scraped, cooked and sliced
½ lb/225 g green beans, cooked and cut into small pieces
1 small cauliflower, broken into flowerets and cooked
½ lb/225 g green peas, cooked
1 medium sized cucumber, unpeeled, skin scored and coarsely chopped

vinaigrette:
1 clove garlic, crushed
½ teaspoon Dijon mustard
salt, freshly ground pepper
2 tablespoons cider vinegar or lemon juice
4 fl oz/125 ml olive or vegetable oil
2 tablespoons parsley, finely chopped
2 tablespoons capers

Combine all the vegetables in a large salad bowl. In a small bowl mix the crushed garlic with the mustard. Season with salt and pepper and stir in the vinegar or lemon juice. Using a fork, beat in the oil until the sauce is thick and well blended. Pour over the vegetables and toss lightly to mix. Garnish with the parsley and capers.

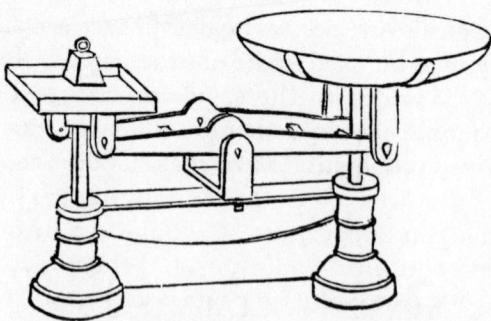

Bread and Cakes

WHOLEMEAL BREAD

To make two loaves

1 oz/25 g fresh yeast or ½ oz/15 g dried yeast
1 tablespoon Demerara or light brown sugar
8 fl oz/250 ml lukewarm water
10 oz/275 g wholemeal flour
4 oz/100 g white bread flour
1 teaspoon salt
1 oz/30 g butter softened at room temperature
1 large egg, lightly beaten
glaze – 1 small egg, lightly beaten with
½ teaspoon salt

In a small bowl combine the yeast and sugar with 4 fl oz/125 ml lukewarm water. Leave in a warm, draught-free place until bubbly, about 15 minutes.

In a large bowl sift together the wholemeal and plain flour with the salt. Rub in the butter with the fingertips until the mixture resembles a coarse meal. Make a well in the centre and add the yeast and the egg and about 4 fl oz/125 ml lukewarm water. Mix thoroughly with a wooden spoon to make a soft but not sticky dough. Add more plain flour if necessary. Turn the dough out on to a lightly floured board and knead it until it is smooth and elastic, about 10–15 minutes. Oil the bowl lightly, form the dough into a ball and roll it in the bowl to coat it very lightly, cover with a damp cloth and put into a draught-free place to rise until doubled in bulk about 1½ hours. An oven heated to its lowest setting for 2 minutes and then switched off is ideal. When the dough has risen, cut it in half and form each half into a 12 inch/30 cm long cylinder. Place on a lightly oiled baking sheet, cover with the cloth, and leave in the oven to rise again until doubled, about 1 hour. Using a very sharp knife, or a razor blade slash the loaves diagonally in 3 places. Brush with the egg glaze and bake in a preheated moderate oven (400°F/200°C/gas 6) for about 25 minutes or until the loaves are browned and sound hollow when tapped on the bottom with the knuckles.

If the bread is to be used for sandwiches form it into a single loaf and put it into a greased 9 inch/23 cm bread tin. Cover with a damp cloth and let it rise in a warm draught-free place until it has again doubled in bulk, about 1½ hours. Brush with the egg mixture and bake in a preheated moderate oven (375°F/190°C/gas 5) for 35–40 minutes, or until the loaf is golden brown and the bottom sounds hollow when tapped with the knuckles. Remove the loaf from the tin and let it cool on a wire rack.

PEANUT BREAD

This is an attractive quick bread to make when time is short and something special is needed.

     ½ lb/225 g bread flour
     ½ lb/ 225 g light brown sugar
     1 tablespoon baking powder
     ½ teaspoon salt

    6 oz/175 g roasted peanuts, finely ground
    8 fl oz/225 ml milk
    1 large egg, lightly beaten
    2 oz/50 g butter, melted and cooled

Sift the flour, sugar, baking powder and salt into a large
bowl with the peanuts. In another bowl mix together the
milk and egg and stir in the butter. Blend the egg mixture
into the flour. Butter a cake tin of 3 pint/1.7 litre capacity
and pour in the butter. Bake in a preheated moderate oven
(350°F/180°C/gas 4) for about 50 minutes, or until a cake
tester inserted in the middle comes out clean. Let the bread
cool for 5 minutes, then turn it out on to a rack to finish
cooling. Serve sliced, with or without butter.

OATMEAL BREAD

This bread has a slightly chewy, crunchy texture with a
good, rather nutty flavour.

Makes 1 loaf

    1 oz/25 g dry yeast or 2 oz/50 g fresh yeast
    1 tablespoon honey
    4 fl oz/125 ml lukewarm water
    11 oz/300 g wholemeal flour
    3 oz/75 g rolled oats
    1 teaspoon salt
    1 large egg, lightly beaten
    4 fl oz/125 ml water

In a bowl combine the yeast, honey, and lukewarm water
and mix thoroughly. Put into a warm, draught-free place
for about 15 minutes or until bubbly.

In a large bowl combine the flour, oats and salt. Make a
well in the centre and add the egg and the yeast mixture.
Mix, using a wooden spoon or the hands, adding the water
as necessary. Knead the mixture in the bowl then turn on
to a lightly floured surface and knead until the dough is

smooth and elastic, about 10–15 minutes. Form into a ball. Oil the bowl lightly and cover the dough very lightly with oil. Cover the bowl with a damp cloth and put into a warm, draught-free place for the dough to rise. An oven previously heated for 2 minutes at its lowest setting is good for this. Let the dough rise until doubled in bulk, about 2 hours. Turn out on to a floured board and knead the dough for a minute or two then shape it into a loaf. Place the loaf into a 2 lb/1 litre buttered bread tin, cover with a damp cloth and leave in a warm draft-free place to rise until again doubled in bulk, about 2 hours. Bake in a preheated moderate oven (350°F/180°C/gas 4) for 1 hour, or until nicely browned and the bottom sounds hollow when tapped with the knuckles. Turn out on to a wire rack and cool.

BRAN BREAD

Nothing is higher in fibre than bran. It gives this loaf a lovely mellow flavour.

Makes 1 loaf

> ½ oz/15 g dry yeast, or 1 oz/25 g fresh yeast
> 1 tablespoon Demerara or light brown sugar
> 8 fl oz/225 ml lukewarm water
> 2½ oz/65 g durun wheat bran
> 12½ oz/350 g bread flour
> 1½ teaspoons salt
> 2 tablespoons vegetable oil
> 1 egg

In a small bowl combine the yeast, sugar and lukewarm water mixing thoroughly. Stand in a warm place for about 15 minutes or until the mixture is foamy. If the yeast has not started to bubble by that time, it is probably too old to be active. Begin again with fresher yeast.

In a large bowl mix together the bran, bread flour and 1 teaspoon of the salt. Make a well in the centre and pour in the yeast mixture. Add the oil and mix with a wooden spoon. Knead for a minute or two in the bowl adding a little extra flour if the mixture seems too wet. Turn out on to a lightly floured surface and knead until the dough is smooth and elastic, about 10 minutes. Form the dough into a ball. Oil the bowl lightly, add the dough and turn it about to coat it with oil. Cover the bowl with a damp cloth and put into a warm, draught-free place to rise until doubled in bulk, about 1½ hours. An oven heated to its lowest setting for 2 minutes then turned off, is excellent.

Turn the risen dough on to a lightly floured surface and knead it again for about 4 minutes. Form it into a loaf and put it into a greased 9 inch/23 cm bread tin. Cover with a damp cloth and put it into the turned off oven to rise until it has again doubled in bulk, about 1½ hours.

Preheat the oven to 375°F/190°C/gas 5. Beat the egg with the remaining salt. Using a very sharp knife, or a razor blade, slash the top of the risen loaf diagonally in 3 or 4 places. Brush lightly all over with the egg mixture and bake in the middle of the oven for 35–40 minutes, or until the loaf is golden brown and the bottom sounds hollow when tapped with the knuckles. Remove the loaf from the tin and let it cool on a wire rack.

CHAPATI

India has a number of breads (Roti) that are traditionally made at home. They are easy to make, delicious to eat, wholesome in their ingredients and high in fibre. They are made from whole-grain flour.

Serves 6

12 oz/350 g wholemeal flour
4 oz/100 g plain flour
1 teaspoon salt
water
butter

Sift all the flour and the salt into a large bowl. With a wooden spoon mix in enough water to make a fairly stiff dough. Turn the dough out on to a lightly floured surface and knead thoroughly until it is smooth and elastic, about 10 minutes. Return the dough to the bowl, cover with a damp cloth and leave in a warm place for about 3 hours. Knead the dough thoroughly again, for about 5 minutes. Cut off pieces of dough about the size of a small egg and form into balls. Roll out each ball into a circle with a rolling pin until it is as thin as possible. Heat an ungreased griddle and cook the chapatis, one by one for about 20 seconds, then turn and cook until light spots appear on the top side. Turn again and cook until the chapati puffs up and browns. Butter lightly and keep warm. Serve as soon as possible.

POORI

Serves 6

12 oz/350 g wholemeal flour
4 oz/100 g plain flour
1 teaspoon salt
1 oz butter, cut into small bits
water
oil or vegetable shortening for deep frying

Sift all the flour and the salt into a large bowl. Rub the butter into the flour with the fingertips until it resembles coarse meal. Add enough water, stirring with a wooden spoon, to make a fairly stiff dough. Turn the dough out on to a lightly floured surface and knead until it is smooth and pliable, about 10 15 minutes. Return the dough to the bowl and cover with a damp cloth. Leave in a warm place for about 1 hour. Knead well again and roll into pieces the size of a small walnut. Roll these out into circles about 3 inches/7.5 cm in diameter. Fry these one by one in deep hot fat. While cooking press the poori gently under the fat with the back of a spoon using a circular motion to press the entire surface. It will puff out. Turn and cook the bread until it is light brown on both sides. Drain on paper towels and serve as soon as possible.

BANANA BREAD

Bananas and wholemeal flour combine to give this tea bread a high fibre content and a delicious flavour.

Makes 1 loaf cake

> 4 oz/100 g butter
> 4 oz/100 g Demerara, or light brown sugar
> 1 large egg
> 4 oz/100 g plain flour
> 4 oz/100 g wholemeal flour
> 2 teaspoons baking powder
> ½ teaspoon salt
> ½ teaspoon ground allspice
> ½ teaspoon freshly grated nutmeg
> 2 large, ripe bananas, weighing about 1 lb/450 g
> 3 oz/75 g sultanas
> 2 oz/50 g walnuts, coarsely chopped

Cream the butter and sugar together in a bowl until light and fluffy. Beat in the egg, mixing thoroughly. Sift the flours, baking powder, salt, allspice and nutmeg into another bowl. In a small bowl mash the bananas and add to the egg and butter mixture with the sultanas and walnuts. Beat this into the sifted ingredients until the batter is well blended. Pour into a buttered cake tin of 3 pint/1.7 litre capacity and bake in a preheated, moderate oven (350°F/

180°C/gas 4) for about 1 hour, or until a cake tester comes out clean.

Serve, sliced, with stewed fruit for dessert, or buttered or with jam for breakfast or with tea.

BRAN, BRAZIL NUT AND APRICOT CAKE

This cake is delicious by itself, but it also makes a splendid accompaniment to Palette of Dried Fruits (page 94).

Serves 8

> 4 oz/100 g dried apricots
> 1 oz/25 g durum wheat bran
> 3 oz/75 g plain flour
> 2 oz/50 g Brazil nuts, finely ground
> 4 oz/100 g Demerara, or light brown sugar
> ¼ teaspoon salt
> 1 teaspoon baking powder
> 2 fl oz/50 ml vegetable oil
> 2 fl oz/50 ml milk
> 3 large eggs, separated
> ¼ teaspoon cream of tartar

Put the apricots into a small bowl with warm water to cover and let them soak for 20 minutes. Drain, pat them dry with paper towels and chop them coarsely. The pieces should be about the size of currants.

In a large bowl sift together the bran, flour, nuts, sugar, salt and baking powder. Fold in the apricots.

In another bowl beat together the vegetable oil and milk. Beat the egg yolks into the oil and milk mixture, then stir into the dry mixture.

In a large bowl beat the egg whites with the cream of tartar until they stand in peaks. Stir a quarter of the whites into the cake batter. Fold the remaining whites into the batter gently but thoroughly. Pour into a greased tube tin or a deep cake tin (2¼ pt/1.3 litre) size. Bake in a preheated, moderate oven (350°F/180°C/gas 4) for 1 hour or until a cake tester comes out clean. Remove the cake to a wire rack and let it cool in the tin for about 30 minutes, then turn it out of the tin on to the rack to finish cooling.

SWEET POTATO CAKE

White sweet potatoes are available in many street markets selling tropical vegetables and in supermarkets. They make a superb cake as well as being a most attractive substitute for rice, or potatoes with a main course. They can be boiled or baked and served with a little butter or can be transformed into cake.

Makes 1 loaf cake

> 2 lb/900 g white sweet potatoes, peeled and sliced
> 1 oz/25 g butter
> 6 oz/175 g Demerara, or brown sugar
> 4 eggs
> 6 fl oz/175 ml milk, or coconut milk
> 1 teaspoon ground allspice
> ½ teaspoon salt
> 2 teaspoons baking powder

Put the sweet potatoes to cook with water to cover and simmer until they are tender, about 20 minutes. Drain and mash. Transfer the potatoes to a bowl and while they are still warm mix in the butter and sugar. Beat in the eggs, one by one. Add the milk, stirring to mix. Mix together the allspice, salt and baking powder and add to the batter, mixing thoroughly. Pour the batter into a buttered 9 by 5 inch/23 by 12.5 cm cake tin and bake in a preheated moderate oven (350°F/180°C/gas 4) for 1 hour or until a cake tester comes out clean. Allow to cool for 10 minutes in the pan then turn on to a cake rack to finish cooling.

PEANUT CAKE

Every now and then a slice of cake makes a pleasant addition to the day's eating. This cake is good for one as well as tasting good.

 half lb/225 g plain flour
1half teaspoons each baking powder and baking soda
6 oz/175 g roasted peanuts, finely ground
half lb/225 g butter, softened at room temperature
half lb/ 225 g Demerara, or light brown sugar
3 eggs, separated
6 fl oz/175 ml soured cream

Into a large bowl sift together the flour, baking powder, and baking soda with the ground peanuts. In another bowl cream together the butter and sugar until it is light and fluffy. Add the egg yolks, one by one, beating well after each addition. Beat in the soured cream. Combine the batter with the flour. Beat the egg whites in a large bowl until they stand in firm peaks. Stir a quarter of the whites into the batter, then fold the remaining whites into the mixture gently but thoroughly.

Butter an 8 inch/20 cm round cake tin and pour in the batter. Bake in a preheated moderate oven (350°F/180°C/ gas 4) for about 1 hour or until a cake tester inserted in the centre comes out clean. Turn the cake out on to a rack, and prick it all over. Spoon hot orange syrup over the cake and let it cool.

To make Orange Syrup

4 oz/125 g Demerara or light brown sugar
3 fl oz/75 ml orange juice
grated rind 1 large orange

In a small saucepan combine the sugar and orange juice and cook, stirring, over low heat until the sugar has dissolved completely. Stir in the orange rind and pour the mixture over the cake. Allow to cool on the rack before serving.

Desserts

PALETTE OF DRIED FRUITS

Dried fruit is rich in fibre though it is not particularly low in calories. Arranged on a decorative platter, or served individually on dessert plates, this looks attractive and tastes delicious. Serve with Bran, Brazil Nut and Apricot Cake (page 91).

Serves 8

4 oz/100 g dried apricots
4 oz/100 g dried peaches
4 oz/100 g dried pears
4 oz/100 g pitted prunes
4 oz/100 g dried quinces (if available)
4 oz/100 g dried apple rings
dry white wine
dry red wine
demerara sugar
granulated sugar
2 tablespoons lemon juice
dried peel of 1 orange

1 oz/25 g toasted, flaked almonds (optional)

Soak the fruits in separate bowls in cold water to cover until they have plumped up, about 1 hour. Drain thoroughly. Cook each fruit in a separate saucepan. Put the apricots, peach and pears to cook with 2 tablespoons Demerara sugar, 8 fl oz/225 ml dry white wine and a 1 inch/2.5 cm piece of dried orange peel. Simmer until the fruit is tender, about 15 minutes. Discard the peel. Purée each fruit separately in a blender or food processor using as much of the cooking liquid as necessary for a purée that will hold its shape in a spoon.

Cook the prunes and quinces separately with sugar, orange peel and dry red wine until tender, then purée. Cook the apple rings in water with 2 tablespoons granulated sugar and the lemon juice. Purée as with the other fruit.

To toast the almonds spread them on a baking sheet and toast in a preheated 300°F/150°C/gas 2 oven until lightly browned, about 10 minutes.

Arrange the apple purée in the centre of a decorative platter and surround it with piles of the other fruit, keeping the fruits separate as on an artist's palette. Sprinkle the apple with flaked almonds if liked. Serve slightly chilled.

Serve with slices of Bran, Brazil Nut and Apricot Cake.

FRUIT COMPOTE

Fresh fruit is high in fibre, so is dried fruit. Together they make a light and delicious dessert, and one that is versatile too as different combinations of dried and fresh fruits can be used, taking advantage of seasonal fruits.

Serves 6

- 4 oz/125 g dried apricots, or pears, or peaches, thinly sliced
- 4 oz/125 g pitted prunes, thinly sliced
- 4 fl oz/125 ml honey
- 3 tablespoons lemon juice
- 2 lb/900 g mixed fresh fruit such as raspberries, strawberries, blackberries, chopped pitted plums, peeled and chopped fresh pineapple, black or red currants, etc
- 3 tablespoons Grand Marnier, Curaçao, or Kirsch (optional)

Put the apricots and prunes into a serving bowl and mix with the honey and lemon juice. Refrigerate for 2 hours. When ready to use gently fold in the fresh fruits and, if liked, pour over the liqueur. Serve immediately.

BLACK FRUIT SALAD

Blackberries are delicious in blackberry pie. They are also delicious if combined with other black fruits like black grapes, black cherries, blackcurrants, purple plums, and any others in season. Rinse and pick over the assorted fruit, about 3 lb/1.4 kg for 6, and remove any seeds or pits if necessary and lightly toss the fruit with a little sugar. Refrigerate until ready to serve. A little liquor may be poured over the fruit to macerate in the refrigerator if liked, and it may be served with cream, plain or whipped, if liked, or with plain yoghurt.

Black Fruit and Red Fruit may be combined in a salad. Raspberries make an admirable addition to a black fruit salad.

Instead of cream, nibble from a bowl of nuts.

Stewed fruits, lightly chilled, and served either with plain yoghurt or the appropriate fruit yoghurt make a light but thoroughly satisfying dessert, with a gratifying amount of fibre.

STUFFED BAKED APPLES

Serves 4

    4 large, firm apples
    4 fl oz/125 ml honey
    2 oz/50 g sultanas, or seedless raisins
    4 whole walnuts
    cinnamon or cloves, ground (optional)

Core the apples carefully so as not to break the skin. Pour the honey into the cavity, stuff with the raisins and top with a walnut broken into halves. If liked add a pinch of cinnamon or clove to the raisins or sultanas.

Butter a baking dish and arrange the apples in it. Pour in about 8 fl oz/225 ml water. Bake the apples in a preheated moderate oven (350°F/180°C/gas 4) for about 30 minutes, or until the apples are tender. Baste with the syrup in the dish and serve.

CARROT PUDDING

The addition of a little rum turns this fibre-rich dessert into a party dish.

Serves 4 to 6

    6 oz/175 g seedless raisins
    4 fl oz/125 ml light rum
    2 ozs/50 g butter
    2 oz/50 g Demerara sugar, or light brown sugar
    8 oz/225 ml carrots, trimmed, scraped and finely grated
    4 ozs/100 g wholemeal flour
    2 teaspoons baking powder

1 teaspoon ground allspice
½ teaspoon salt
2 large eggs, well beaten

Put the raisins to soak in a small bowl with the rum. In another bowl cream together the butter and sugar. Add the grated carrots, raisins and rum, mixing well. In a large bowl silt together the flour, baking powder, allspice and salt. Add the carrot mixture. Fold in the eggs gently but thoroughly. Pour the batter into a greased 2 pint/1.1 litre soufflé dish and bake in a preheated moderate oven (350°F/180°C/gas 4) for about 30 minutes or until a cake tester comes out clean.

The rum may be omitted and the raisins soaked in plain warm water, if preferred.

Sauces, Pickles and Savouries

SWEET RED PEPPER SAUCE

This is a very fresh-tasting sauce and can be used with lots of dishes. It is good with any of the pulses (dried beans, lentils), with meat, poultry or fish and with Toad-in-the-Hole.

    4 fl oz/125 ml olive oil
    1 lb/450 g tomatoes, peeled and chopped
    2 cloves garlic, crushed (optional)
    ½ teaspoon cayenne pepper or hot paprika (optional)
    ½ teaspoon oregano
    salt
    4 red peppers, seeded, peeled and finely chopped

Heat the oil in a large saucepan and add all the ingredients. Cook, stirring from time to time with a wooden spoon until the sauce is thick and well blended. Serve hot. Makes about 1½ pints/800 ml.

If no red ripe tomatoes are available fresh, use tinned Italian tomatoes and simmer the tomatoes in the oil for 5 minutes without the other ingredients to reduce the liquid.

To peel the peppers, char them over a gas flame or under a grill, put them into a plastic or brown paper bag for 30 minutes and rinse off the skin under cold running water.

FRESH TOMATO SAUCE

This easy to make tomato sauce retains all the fresh flavour of the ripe fruit. If tomatoes are out of season make do with tinned Italian plum tomatoes.

    1 tablespoon olive or vegetable oil
    1 medium onion, finely chopped
    1 large clove garlic, chopped (optional)
    1 lb/450 g tomatoes, peeled and chopped
    salt, freshly ground pepper
    1 tablespoon chopped fresh herbs such as basil, parsley
        or coriander or use 1 teaspoon dried herbs such as
        thyme, marjoram, savory, oregano

Heat the oil in a saucepan and add the onion. Sauté over moderate heat until the onion is soft. Add the garlic if using and sauté for 1 minute longer. Add the tomatoes, season to taste with salt and pepper and simmer, uncovered, for 10 minutes. Stir in the herb and simmer for 5 minutes longer to blend the flavours.

If using tinned Italian plum tomatoes add a pinch of sugar and 1 tablespoon tomato purée.

PESTO
Basil and Pine Kernel Sauce

Basil is easy to grow from seed in a pot or in the garden, and greengrocers often have pots of well established plants available. Pine kernels are available in health food shops and often in groceries. Pesto takes only minutes to make in a blender or food processor and makes a delicious main dish when tossed with whole wheat spaghetti.

Serves 4 as a main course, 6–8 as a first course

> 2 oz/50 g fresh basil leaves, coarsely chopped
> 1 oz/25 g pine kernels
> 1 oz/25 g freshly grated Parmesan cheese
> 2 cloves garlic, or to taste
> 3 fl oz/75 ml olive oil
> ½ teaspoon salt
> 1 lb/450 g whole wheat spaghetti, freshly cooked

Combine all the ingredients, except the spaghetti, in a food processor or a blender and reduce it to a paste. Toss it with the hot spaghetti and serve immediately.

Variation: Serve with baked potato instead of spaghetti.

PEANUT SAUCE

> 1 oz/30 ml butter or vegetable oil
> 1 medium onion, finely chopped
> 1 clove garlic, crushed (optional)
> 3 oz/75 g finely ground peanuts
> 2 teaspoons brown sugar
> 1 teaspoon lime or lemon juice
> 1 fresh hot red pepper, seeded and minced, or hot pepper sauce to taste
> salt
> 8 fl oz/225 ml coconut milk (page 25)

Heat the butter in a small frying pan and sauté the onion and garlic until soft and golden. Add the peanuts, sugar, lime or lemon juice, hot pepper or sauce and salt to taste. Stir to mix. Add the coconut milk and cook over low heat, stirring, until the sauce is thick and smooth.

Serve the sauce over vegetables or hardboiled eggs. It is

particularly good with plainly cooked cabbage.

OKRA PICKLE

This is an easily made pickle that is pleasant with cold meats, poultry or curries.

Makes 1¾ pint/1 litre

> 8 oz/225 g small, young okra
> 2 tablespoons minced garlic
> 2 tablespoons minced fresh ginger root
> 2 tablespoons finely chopped fresh coriander
> ¾ pint/450 ml white vinegar or cider vinegar
> 4 oz/100 g brown sugar
> ½ teaspoon turmeric

Rince the okra. Trim if necessary but do not cut off the tops. In a bowl combine the garlic, ginger root and coriander. Cut a 1 inch/2.5 cm slit in the side of each okra pod and stuff with about ½ teaspon of the garlic mixture. Put the stuffed okra into Kilner or other preserving jars. Jam jars can be used, but cover with paper, not metal tops because of the corrosive action of the vinegar.

Combine the vinegar, sugar and turmeric in a saucepan and bring to the boil. Simmer, stirring, until the sugar is dissolved. Pour into the jars to within ½ inch/2.5 ml of the tops. Seal and stand at room temperature overnight them refrigerate for 1 week before using. It will keep for a further two weeks in the refrigerator.

TOASTED CHICKPEAS

This is an attractive cocktail nibble and makes a change from the more usual peanuts.

1 lb/450 g chickpeas
1 teaspoon salt
4 fl oz/125 ml vegetable oil
Cayenne pepper

Wash and pick over the chickpeas and put into a saucepan with cold water to cover. Bring to the boil and simmer, covered for 5 minutes. Let stand for 1 hour. Drain, cover with fresh water, add the salt and simmer for 1 hour or until the chickpeas are tender. Drain and let them dry.

Heat the oil in a large frying pan and sauté the chickpeas until they are golden brown. Drain on kitchen towels and sprinkle with cayenne pepper.

Tinned chickpeas can be used in which case rinse and dry them, then fry them in the oil and sprinkle with the hot pepper.

CHICKPEAS AND SESAME PASTE

This is the famous Middle Eastern Hummus bi Tahini. It is impossible to leave out anything so easy to make, so good to eat and so rich in fibre.

½ lb/225 g chickpeas, cooked in the usual way (page 34)
1 or 2 cloves garlic, or more to taste, crushed
3 fl oz/75 ml lemon juice, or more to taste
salt to taste
4 fl oz/125 ml tahini
1 tablespoon parsley, finely chopped

Combine all the ingredients in a blender or food processor and reduce them to a purée. Add a little water if the purée is too thick. It should be the consistency of mayonnaise. Taste and add more lemon juice or garlic as liked. Sprinkle with parsley and serve as a dip with pitta bread.

Traditionally the dip is garnished with a tablespoon of olive oil mixed with a teaspoon of paprika, drizzled over the parsley. It looks very pretty.

PEANUT BUTTER

Nothing could be easier than making peanut butter using a food processor or blender and it is possible to get exactly the texture to suit personal taste.

> 1 lb/450 g raw peanuts
> 1 tablespoon peanut oil
> ½ teaspoon salt

Spread the peanuts on a baking sheet and roast in a preheated moderate over (350°F/180°C/gas 4) until they are golden, about 15 minutes. Let them cool then pulverize half the nuts in a food processor or blender until they are very fine. Transfer to a bowl and stir in the peanut oil and salt. Add the remaining nuts to the processor with the ground nuts and process to whatever consistency is preferred. If using a blender, it may be necessary to do this in batches.

Fibre Chart

Fibre can be defined as the edible container in which our food has been packaged by nature. The walls of every cell in plants are made of fibre, and fibre creates the skeleton of plants as bones make the skeletons of animals. Eating the container along with the contents of the package – the skin of the apple, the bran layer round the grain of wheat – gives our digestive system the bulk it needs to do its job.

This chart gives the detailed fibre content of a wide range of foods, useful for those who wish to make a count of the amount of fibre in their diet. However, for those who wish to make a more general assessment, here are simple guidelines.

There is no fibre in meat, fish or poultry, in eggs, dairy products, fat and oils, or in sugars. Much of the fibre is removed from cereals by processing so that white flour, polished rice, white bread, and pasta made from white flour have little fibre. High fibre foods are all the whole grain cereals, bran and wheat germ, pasta made from wholemeal flour, bread made from wholemeal flour and unrefined cereals, nuts and seeds, legumes (beans, peas, lentils), fresh vegetables, root vegetables, and fresh and dried fruits.

Cereals

Quantities found in 4 ounce (100 g) portions

All-Bran	27.9 g
Bran	44 g
Barley	2.2 g
Bread	
bran	6.3 g
brown	5.1 g
white	2.7 g
wholemeal	8.5 g
Corn-on-the-cob	4.7 g
Corn kernels	5.7 g
Cornmeal (maize meal) uncooked	9.3 g
Flour	
brown (80–85%)	7.5 g
plain	3.4 g
self-raising	3.7 g
wholemeal	9.6 g
Oatmeal (raw)	7.0 g
Oatmeal (cooked)	0.8 g
Pasta (all types – uncooked)	
white	3.0 g
wholewheat	10.0 g
Pearl barley	2.2 g
Porridge	0.8 g
Rice brown (uncooked)	5.0 g
white (uncooked)	2.4 g
Soya flour, full fat	11.9 g
Soya flour, low fat	14.3 g

Fruit

Quantities of fibre found in 4 ounce (100 g) portions of fresh and dried fruit, raw unless otherwise noted.

Apples, eating, with skin and	2.0 g
Apples, cooking, baked, stewed	2.0 g

Apricots, fresh	1.9 g
dried, raw	24.0 g
dried, cooked	8.9 g
tinned	1.3 g
Bananas	3.4 g
Blackberries	7.3 g
cooked	6.3 g
Blackcurrants	8.7 g
cooked	7.4 g
tinned	5.0 g
Cherries	1.5 g
cooked	1.2 g
tinned	1.0 g
Cranberries	4.2 g
Currants, dried	6.5 g
Redcurrants	8.2 g
Whitecurrants	6.8 g
cooked	5.8 g
Damsons	3.7 g
cooked	3.2 g
Dates, stoned	8.7 g
Dates, with stones	7.5 g
Figs	2.5 g
dried	18.5 h
dried, cooked	10.3 g
Gooseberries	3.2 g
cooked	2.7 g
Grapes	0.9 g
Greengages	2.5 g
cooked	2.1 g
Lemons	5.2 g
Loganberries	6.2 g
Lychees	0.5 g
Mandarin oranges, tinned	0.3 g
Mangoes	1.5 g
Melons (cantaloupe)	1.0 g
(honeydew)	0.9 g
Mulberries	1.7 g
Nectarines	2.2 g

Olives (in brine with stones)	3.5 g
Olives (without stones)	4.4 g
Oranges	1.5 g
Passion fruit, whole	6.7 g
Peaches	1.2 g
dried, raw	14.3 g
dried, cooked	5.3 g
tinned	1.0 g
Pears	1.7 g
cooked	2.5 g
tinned	1.7 g
Pineapple	1.2 g
tinned	0.9 g
Plantain, green raw	5.8 g
boiled	6.4 g
ripe, fried	5.8 g
Plums, raw and cooked	2.0 g
Prunes, raw	13.4 g
cooked	7.4 g
Quinces	6.4 g
Raisins, dried, seedless	6.8 g
Raspberries	7.4 g
Rhubarb	2.6 g
cooked	2.4 g
Strawberries	2.2 g
Sultanas	7.0 g
Tangerines	1.3 g

Nuts
Quantities found in 4 ounce/100 g portions, raw, shelled.

Almonds	14.3 g
Almond paste	6.4 g
Barcelona nuts	10.3 g
Brazil nuts	9.0 g
Chestnuts	6.8 g
Coconut, dessicated	23.5 g
cooked	2.1 g

Coconut, fresh	13.6 g
Hazel nuts (cob nuts, filberts)	6.1 g
Peanuts (ground nuts) raw or roasted	8.1 g
Peanut butter	7.6 g
Pecans	5.2 g
Walnuts	5.2 g

Legumes (Beans, etc)

Quantities of fibre found in 4 ounce (100 g) portions of dried or fresh legumes, cooked unless otherwise stated.

Baked Beans in Tomato Sauce	7.3 g
Beansprouts	3.0 g
Broad beans	4.2 g
Butter beans	5.1 g
Chickpeas	7.5 g
Green beans, French	3.2 g
Green beans, runner	3.4 g
Haricot beans	7.5 g
Kidney beans (tinned)	6.8 g
Lentils	3.7 g
Mung beans	6.4 g
Peas, fresh or frozen	9.1 g
Peas (tinned)	6.2 g
Red kidney, black kidney, pinto beans	7.1 g
Soyabeans	12.0 g
Split peas	5.1 g

Vegetables, root and green (excluding beans)

Quantities of fibre found in 4 ounce (100 g) portions, raw unless otherwise stated.

Asparagus, cooked	0.8 g
Aubergine	2.5 g
Avocado	2.0 g
Beetroot, cooked	2.5 g

Broccoli, cooked	4.1 g
Brussels sprouts, cooked	2.9 g
Cabbage (red, Savoy, spring, white)	3.4 g
cooked	2.8 g
Carrots, raw and cooked	3.0 g
Cauliflower	2.1 g
cooked	1.8 g
Celery	1.8 g
cooked	2.2 g
Celeriac, cooked	4.9 g
Horseradish	8.3 g
sauce	3.0 g
Leeks, cooked	3.9 g
Lettuce	1.5 g
Marrow, cooked	0.6 g
Mushrooms	2.5 g
cooked	4.0 g
Mustard and cress	3.7 g
Okra	3.2 g
Onions, raw and cooked	1.3 g
Parsley	9.1 g
Parsnips, cooked	2.5 g
Potatoes, baked in jackets	2.5 g
boiled	1.0 g
Potato crisps	11.9 g
Pumpkin	0.5 g
Radishes	1.0 g
Spinach	6.3 g
Spring greens, cooked	1.1 g
Spring onions	3.1 g
Swedes, cooked	2.8 g
Sweet Potatoes, cooked	2.3 g
Turnips, cooked	2.2 g
Watercress	3.3 g
Yam, cooked	3.9 g

INDEX

Apples, stuffed baked 97

Bananas, boiled green 45
  bread 90
  with okra and prawns 20
Barley and mushroom casserole 71
Beans 57–64
  and cabbage soup 8
  baked beans 64
  black bean soup 9
  black kidney beans 61
  caldo gallego 12
  with corn and pumpkin 62
  flageolets with lamb 32
  green beans with mushrooms 42
  green beans with water chestnuts 41
  haricot beans and rice 66
  Mexico-style 60
  pot beans 57
  refried beans 59
  and rice 66, 67
  in salads 21, 73–77
  soya beans, mushrooms and peppers 63
  Venezuelan black beans 61
Beef and cornmeal pie 39
Black fruit salad 96
Bran, brazil nut and apricot cake 91
Bread, banana 90
  bran 87
  chapati 88
  oatmeal 86
  peanut 85
  poori 89
  wholemeal 84
Broccoli with spinach or walnuts 44
Brussel sprouts with chestnuts 45
Bulgur see Cracked wheat

Cakes 90–93
  bran, brazil nut and apricot 90
  peanut 92
  sweet potato 92
Carrot pudding 97
Carrots and leeks, julienne 40
Cassoulet 29
Chapati 88
Chestnuts with Brussel sprouts 45
Chicken in peanut sauce 35
Chickpeas and apricot salad 82
  puréed 69
  and sesame paste 103

  toasted 102
  with tripe 34
  and tomato salad 81
Coconut rice and beans 67
Corn with okra and tomatoes 48
  and tomato soup 17
Cornmeal with beef 39
  with coconut milk and fish 25
  with sausages 38
  and young okra 46
Cracked wheat 70
  and apricot salad 83

Dal 68
Desserts 94–98
  baked apples, stuffed 97
  black fruit salad 96
  carrot pudding 97
  dried fruits, palette of 94
  fruit compote 95

Feijoada completa 31
Fennel and pea purée 46
Fibre, charts 105–110
  in the diet 6–7
Fish with cornmeal and coconut milk 25
  curried with peanuts 23
  kedgeree 24
  pie with sweet potato topping 27
  prawns with brown rice 26
  prawns with banana and okra 20
  tuna and bean salad 21
  tuna stuffed potatoes 22
Flageolets with lamb 32
Fruit compote 95

Hummus 103

Kedgeree 24

Lamb, braised leg with flageolets 33
Leeks and carrots, julienne 40
  sautéed 41
Lentil and apricot salad 83
  and apricot soup 10
  purée 67
  soup 11

Maize 25 see also Cornmeal
Mangetout and mushroom salad 78
Millet 69
Minestrone 14

Mushroom and barley casserole 71
  and mangetout salad 78
  peppers and soyabeans 63

Oatmeal bread 86
Okra with aubergine and tomatoes 47
  and bananas and prawns 20
  with cornmeal 46
  curried 49
  pickle 102

Palette of dried fruits 94
Peas and curried potatoes 55
  and fennel purée 46
  soup 16
Peanut bread 85
  butter 104
  and curried fish 23
  cake 92
  and rabbit ragoût 36
  sauce 101
  soup 19
Peppers, stuffed green 49
Pesto 100
Poori 89
Pot beans 57
Potatoes baked 52
  baked with sorrel chiffonnade 54
  caviar 53
  curried, and peas 55
  new potatoes and spinach 43
  and tuna stuffing 22
Prawns with brown rice 26
  with okra and banana 20
Pumpkin with beans and corn 62

Rabbit and peanut ragoût 36
Rice, bean and vegetable salad 74
  and black haricot beans 66
  brown rice 65
  brown rice and prawns 26
  coconut rice and red kidney beans 67
  kedgeree 24
  oriental salad 80
  peanut rice 65

Salads 72–83
  bean 76
  bean, rice and vegetable 74
  chickpea and tomato 81
  four bean 73
  herbed vegetable 79

  mangetout and mushroom 78
  mixed vegetable 83
  okra 78
  oriental rice 80
  soyabean 77
  tuna and kidney bean 21
  warm chickpea and apricot 82
  wholemeal spaghetti 72
Salsify and scorzonera 42
Sauces, fresh tomato 100
  peanut 101
  pesto 100
  sweet red pepper 99
Sausages with cornmeal topping 38
Sorrel chiffonnade 55
  chiffonnade with butter 55
  soup 15
Soups 8–19
  bean and cabbage 8
  black bean 9
  caldo gallego 12
  chilled: carrot 18
    corn and tomato 17
    green summer 17
    peanut 19
  fresh pea 16
  lentil 11
  lentil and apricot 10
  minestrone 14
  sorrel 15
  turnip 16
Soyabeans, mushrooms and peppers 63
Spinach with mushrooms 44
  with new potatoes 43
  with walnuts 44
Sweet potato cake 92
Sweet red pepper sauce 99
Syrup, orange 93

Toad-in-the-hole 37
Tomato sauce 100
Tripe with chickpeas 34
Tuna stuffed potatoes 22
  and bean salad 21
Turnip soup 16

Vegetable medley 50
  platter 51
  salads 79, 83

Water chestnuts with green beans 41